THE MYSTERY
OF THE
CHURCH

THE MYSTERY
OF THE
CHURCH

by William Bush

REGINA

SALISBURY, MA

1999

ISBN 0-9649141-7-4

Cover Photo: S. Vitalis Emperor Justina (6th Cetury), Ravenna, Italy. Used by permission.

Regina Orthodox Press
PO Box 5288 Salisbury MA 01952 USA
Toll Free 800 636 2470
Fax 978 462 5079 non-USA 978 463 0730
www.reginaorthodoxpress.com

TABLE OF CONTENTS

BIOGRAPHY

Born a Southern Baptist in 1929 in Florida, William Bush embraced Anglo-Catholicism at age 20. In 1955 an unforeseen encounter with a holy Russian woman in Paris revealed to him that Orthodoxy too might be embraced by those who were not born Orthodox. Three years residence in Paris (1956-1959) to write his Sorbonne thesis followed this decisive encounter, allowing him to steep himself in the Orthodoxy of Paris's sizeable Russian colony. He did not, however, out of obedience, seek admission into the Church before a ten-year wait expired in 1967 when, at age 38, he was received into the Greek Church.

Professor Emeritus of the University of Western Ontario, William Bush began his academic career in 1959 with seven years at Duke University before immigrating in 1966 with his English wife and four children to London, Ontario, where he had been named Professor of French. His authoritative volumes in French and English both on the French Catholic writer, Georges Bernanos, and on the sixteen blessed Carmelite martyrs of Compiègne are recognized internationally.

In 1977 William Bush was co-founder of the English-language Holy Transfiguration Orthodox Parish (Antiochian) in London, Ontario, where he serves as chanter.

CHAPTER I

THE MYSTERY OF "THE" ORTHODOX CHURCH

Those outside the Orthodox Church often wonder how their Orthodox friends can speak, so unabashedly and with no explanation whatsoever, of belonging to "the" Orthodox Church. Is Orthodoxy not universally known for its unending nationalistic and jurisdictional divisions? Are there not, after all, Greek Orthodox, Russian Orthodox, Antiochian Orthodox and, heaven only knows, how many other kinds of Orthodox churches? Albanian, Bulgarian, Romanian, Serbian, Ukrainian--the list is imposing. How is it conceivable even to speak of "the" Orthodox Church as if it were an entity?

This question is legitimate, reflecting as it does the sins of Orthodox people against their own Church. Immigrants in non-Orthodox lands, they have permitted the duplication of Orthodox bishops in one place because of ethnic differences, each ethnic group wishing to survive with its own distinctive culture. Orthodox canon law, however, strictly forbids such duplication and overlapping of Orthodox hierarchy. Still, canon law is cleverly by-passed by assigning bishops titles of dioceses no longer functioning in the old country. Therefore, in theory if not in practice, not one of several Orthodox bishops found in a given city may, in fact, really be the titular bishop of that city. Though the letter of canon law is thereby preserved, the spirit most certainly is not, leaving outsiders with the impression that the Orthodox Church, as a single, identifiable body of faithful, cannot possibly exist.

In spite of such gross and on-going violations of canon law by groups intent, before all else, on their personal ethnic

1

survival in their new land (and usually with no thought whatsoever of making their own Orthodoxy accessible to the native inhabitants of their new land), Orthodoxy continues to exist. It has even come to be quite generally recognized in the western world as a distinct and identifiable form of Christianity which, it is evident, proves of infinite, unfathomable consolation to her unbending faithful.

Even today and against all odds Orthodoxy continues to bear witness, after two thousand years, to the fullness of the mighty, dynamic power of that Christianity handed down by the Apostles, complete with miracles and wonders, martyrs, saints and confessors. Deeply rooted in a loving intimacy with the risen Christ often astounding outsiders, Orthodoxy's ceaseless prayers for the world and for the race of men make it hard to find her equal in extending hope and consolation to all who draw near to her with fear of God, with love and with faith.

This on-going, dynamic witness of Orthodoxy is proudly accepted by the Orthodox themselves as the never-ending miracle of their faith, sustained by the Holy Spirit. Orthodoxy's claims to be the Church of God thereby seem fully confirmed for the believer. Is not the Holy Spirit ever at work within her, openly manifesting God's great mercy to the world through her? In spite of her many and great sins, men can, and do continue to see her good works, and to glorify God.

The Orthodox insist upon the fact that the Orthodox Church is indeed the depository of the fullness of apostolic Christian truth. They believe this not because they are told it from above, but because of their own experience of partaking of her divine life. This divine life is, of course, that life bestowed upon creation by the coming into this world of Jesus Christ, of Him who said that He came that we might have life *"more abundantly" (Jn 10:10)*. Through Him, the Second Person of the Holy Trinity, Orthodoxy maintains that man, in spite of belonging to a fallen race, nonetheless has the potential, through the power of the Holy Spirit at work within him, of participating in the very life of the Triune God.

ii

The Orthodox Church's continued witness since the first centuries of Christianity has actually been consistent, whatever her appearance to the outsider of lacking a solid, visible worldly foundation on which to base her existence. Orthodoxy claims no quick and easy reference to prove her authenticity, such as a Vatican or a Pope. The ancient Patriarchates of Jerusalem, Antioch, Alexandria and Constantinople, plus those churches in communion with them, continue however to weld the Orthodox faithful together in a common witness to the God-Man Jesus Christ, and to His mighty power to redeem the human race from death. They are also joined in one communion, a communion of which the Pope of Rome himself partook during the first thousand years of Christian history.

From generation to generation this common communion has continued to unite Orthodoxy's faithful in one body of faith and practice. Though a simple fact, it is one just now being discovered by certain non-Orthodox in North America who, out of their love for the things of God, cannot but be impressed by Orthodoxy's long succession of martyrs, saints, confessors and Holy Fathers. Moreover, are Orthodoxy's

3

claims to complete and unbroken authenticity in representing the Church of God through her four ancient patriarchates not historically substantiated by the fact that her martyrs, saints and confessors of the first thousand years of Christian history are shared with the Church of Rome which also still venerates them?

Rome, however, not only sinned against her sister Patriarchates by claiming universal jurisdiction over them, but also thereby sinned even more gravely against the wholeness of the mystery of the Church of God. Paradoxically, separation has inevitably condemned the Roman Church over the last thousand years to evolve into a purely western institution to such an extent that today Orthodoxy seems almost as "foreign" to her faithful as to Protestants. Whatever may be the Vatican's diplomatic status as a world state, the Roman Church has in fact effectively become a provincial, western Christian institution, her fate associated with that of post-Renaissance western civilization. It is that civilization today which sweeps the world with its brutal technology, its merciless laws concerning economic efficiency, and its blind faith in man's supremacy over the universe.

Rather than that universal institution she has so aspired to be, Rome in fact often emerges as an organization of contemporary western European culture, deeply committed to honoring the primacy of science, as it were to make atonement for her condemnation of Galileo in the past. Paradoxically, in her admirable attempts to stand against modern European culture, she still yields to its dictates. Indeed, even when the saints of God are involved, medical tribunals must verify miracles, thereby betraying the Roman Church's overweening desire to be respected of men by submitting the works of God to the standards of western technology. Does repeatedly submitting the Holy Shroud of Turin to tests by non-believers not proclaim this frightening obsession with scientific orientation? For journalists all of this makes very good copy, of course, and seems far more "relevant" than the far greater mystery of some humble, uneducated believer's faith in the virgin birth of Jesus Christ. Scorn of the uneducated and unsophisticated can but follow in the wake of so-called scientific certainty. Little room is left for that God of the Gospels who "*puts down the mighty from their seat and exalts the humble and meek*". (Lk 1:52)

Thus may one say that in spite of her pretension of being, by divine right through the words of Jesus Christ to St. Peter, the "universal Church," Rome has, over the last thousand years, increasingly propagated a peculiarly western, highly clericalist world-view. Ironically, it is this world-view, rather than the Gospel of Christ, that, in the end, has had an incalculable impact on contemporary civilization, underlining the great distance separating the post-Renaissance world-view of Roman Christians from the older, pre-Renaissance and traditional world-view of Orthodox Christians.

iii

The Orthodox Church's experience of history differs radically, of course, from that of the Roman Church. Orthodoxy never knew an obscure period such as "the Dark Ages." She therefore had no need for a "renaissance" of pagan classical culture. At the time Rome was being overrun and laid waste by barbarians, the Orthodox Church in Constantinople was quite relaxed, guarding the classical

5

culture of both Rome and Greece as her own living heritage. Rome, the old Empire's center of the world, was sacked in 410, again in 455, and finally in 476. At this latter date the last Emperor of the Western Empire was deposed, marking, Western historians usually say, "the end of the Roman Empire."

Historians speaking thus of the "end of the Roman Empire" conveniently forget that in 330, almost a century and a half prior to this 476 date, Constantine the Great had actually transferred his seat of government from old Rome to Constantinople, christening it "New Rome." It was there that the administration of the Roman Empire with its old civilization continued, complete with Constantinople's famous Hippodrome and those Roman games the populace so loved.

Following Rome's 476 catastrophe, however, it would be more than three centuries before the old capital of the ruined Western Empire, trying bravely to cope with her terrible reversal of fortune, could finally emerge again with any semblance of order as a temporal power. And it was indeed the Pope of Rome who was best situated to bring all this about through the advent of Charlemagne, a remarkably successful and charismatic warrior-chieftain. Discerning in Charlemagne a genius capable of administering an empire, the Pope summoned him to Rome in 800, and, on Christmas day, crowned him "Emperor of the Holy Roman Empire," thereby launching a rival emperor to stand against the well-established Emperor of "New Rome" in Constantinople.

It was but natural that "New Rome's" patriarch be of especial concern to the Pope. The Patriarch of New Rome, as New Rome itself, could only be viewed by the Bishop of old Rome as a rival to his power. Far more than the more ancient patriarchs of Antioch, Alexandria and Jerusalem, it was New Rome's upstart patriarchate who, so closely associated with the now-Christian Emperor of the old Roman Empire, posed a potential threat to Rome's tenacious ambition to function as supreme arbitrator in all ecclesiastical matters affecting the Church of God.

iv

Though Charlemagne's imperial glory may seem a bit rustic today when compared to the glory of the Emperor of Constantinople, it was a brave effort by the Pope to impose some sort of unity in the West. It was also a mighty bulwark to the Roman pontiff's own temporal ambitions to stand against the power of "New Rome" as embodied in Constantinople. Thanks to Charlemagne, dispersed parts of the western empire were reconquered and Roman Christianity imposed on one vanquished pagan people after another as they received the option of death by the sword or Christian baptism. As an illiterate chieftain-emperor, Charlemagne proved a jarring contrast to his highly literate Byzantine counterpart, firmly ensconced for five centuries already in "New Rome" as the direct descendent of the Caesars. Still, the illiterate Charlemagne's coronation in 800 did bolster the prestige and temporal power of the Pope of Rome, laying the foundation for increasing rivalry and, two and one-half centuries later, the Great Schism of 1054.

Constantinople, from its founding in 330 as a specifically Christian city, had been placed under the protection of the virgin Godbirthgiver. For almost five centuries Constantine's "New Rome" flourished. The pagan cultures of Rome and

Greece were fused with Christianity and transformed. From the beginning, moreover, the Greek language, proud heritage from the vast empire of Alexander the Great, had proven the one truly common language of Rome's far-flung empire.

It was but natural then that Greek would serve in a providential manner as the Apostles' missionary language for disseminating Christianity. Neither the provincial Aramaic of Jesus Christ, nor distant Rome's administrative Latin could have reached so many. That Greek was therefore ordained to triumph, not only as the language of "New Rome's" Orthodox Christianity, but also as the language of the whole Eastern Empire, was inevitable. Latin's death-knell was finally sounded in "New Rome" only in the first half of the seventh century when the Emperor Heraclius I (610-641) decreed that Greek replace Latin in the two domains where it had anachronistically survived: government administration and the army. A generation later the use of Latin had become extinct in the East.

Constantine's "New Rome" was also inevitably steeped in Orthodox Christianity from the beginning. In 325, five years even before the founding of "New Rome," Constantine had summoned the bishops of the Christian Church to an Ecumenical Council at Nicea where he himself, though still unbaptized, held first place of honor. As Emperor of the Roman Empire, he spoke in Latin, even though the deliberations and documents formulated by the Council of Bishops would all be in Greek.

Three hundred eighteen bishops from throughout the Empire assembled there to define the identity of that Christ in whose sign Constantine had conquered, and in whose name many of the 318 bishops had so shortly before suffered imprisonment, tortures, forced labor, maiming and disfigurements. Stumps from which hands or feet had been struck off, cavities left where noses had been cut off or eyes gouged out, marked the sufferings which they, like St. Paul, interpreted as *"the marks of the Lord Jesus"* (Gal 6: 17) given them to bear in their own bodies for love of Him. Paul, Bishop of Neocaesarea, whose inanimate hands were calcified from having had molten metal poured on them and left to cool, was piously sought out by the Emperor himself. In humble veneration the pious, unbaptized Constantine bowed before those hideous, calcified hands and, venerating them as holy relics, remarked, *"I do not tire of kissing hands made dead and lifeless for my Christ."*

The paradoxical image of the Church of God's maimed confessors assembled by imperial order to partake of the glory of mighty Rome's emperor, uncannily foretells the mystical future of Orthodoxy as it still exists in the world today. For the true glory of Orthodoxy at that First Ecumenical Council was in the "marks" on her bishops' mangled bodies rather than in the dazzling splendor of worldly glory surrounding the Emperor of the mighty Rome of the Caesars. Their bodies, in that year 325, bore testimony to their faith that Jesus Christ was God, a faith being disputed and challenged by the teachings of the priest, Arius of Alexandria.

Indeed, Arius and his followers held that the Son, incarnate in Jesus Christ, was not really the *"only begotten Son and Word,"* not really of *"one essence with the Father,"* but a creature, created by God. The Second Person of the Holy Trinity, Arius taught, had most definitely not been *"begotten of His Father before all ages; Light of Light, true God of true God, of one essence with the Father"* as the

Nicean creed was to proclaim. Orthodox Christians understood however that by saying the Son was created by the Father after the beginning, Arius's teaching robbed Christians of its even being possible for their own nature to have been assumed by God Himself in order to make them like Him.

Settling this question concerning the identity of the Son of God was, therefore, the primary matter of business for that First Ecumenical Council. Constantine had called it precisely that it might restore harmony between the warring parties in the Church, so bitterly divided over this question.

That Jesus Christ is the incarnation of the only-begotten Son and Word of God, existing from the beginning with God and, therefore, One with God, has indeed always been the true glory of Orthodoxy. The endless chain of martyrs and confessors who continue to come forward, even today, to suffer for the Orthodox faith as they confess Jesus Christ as their Lord and God is an on-going revelation of that glory. As at the Council of Nicea, the blood of the martyrs remains the surest guarantee of the Church's on-going authenticity, assuring us of the continuation of the Holy Spirit's witness to the fullness of Christian truth in Orthodoxy. Within the mystery of the Church the blood of the martyrs has ever served efficaciously as a bulwark against the unstinted striving of the forces of darkness to stifle the Church of God.

One should never forget moreover that human suffering for the sake of the divinity of Jesus Christ did provide an ever-present backdrop against which the heady, imperial glory of the Eastern Empire's official Orthodoxy was largely played out. Time after time imprisonment, torture and martyrdom were meted out to confessors for the Orthodox faith by a seemingly endless succession of enemies, be it

MYSTERY OF THE CHURCH

Arians, Iconoclasts, Persians, Frankish Crusaders, Turks, or heretical emperors, often in connivance with an ambitious, or heretical patriarch.

Not even that very great hierarch, St. John Chrysostom, Patriarch of Constantinople, whose Divine Liturgy remains to this day the one most frequently used in the Orthodox Church, was spared his martyr's witness. During the struggle in Constantinople accompanying his overthrow, arrest, deportation and death in exile, the sacred waters for the catechumens' baptism at Easter were reddened on Holy Saturday by the blood of those Orthodox vainly defending the great and holy patriarch from his enemies.

All those espoused to Jesus Christ have, of course, been assured by their Lord and God: *"In the world ye shall have tribulation: but be of good cheer; I have overcome the world"* (John 16:33), something much underlined in the eighth and ninth centuries by those numerous confessors who suffered for the holy icons. Though almost totally ignored outside the Orthodox Church, those innumerable martyrdoms for the holy icons constitute a glorious chapter in the chronicles of the appalling sufferings repeatedly demanded of Orthodox Christians to preserve their faith from those in authority over them and pretending to be Orthodox. Indeed, what the Orthodox today celebrate as the official *"triumph over the iconoclasts"* at the Seventh Ecumenical Council in 787 in no way prevented a resurgence of iconoclastic persecution under subsequent emperors in the next century. Faces of the persecutors of Orthodoxy are indeed ever changing, yet they are ever one in somehow assuring, from century to century, that relentless persecution for faith in Jesus Christ as God will always be a given in Orthodox history.

MYSTERY OF THE CHURCH

V

It is hardly surprising then that one discovers, deeply rooted in the Orthodox psyche, a sort of basic expectation that the Church of God will always be under siege. Such an expectation cannot but nurture a profound mistrust of Rome's optimistic and too-visible militancy. With awesome display of her worldly power and glory, she continues her attempts to impose on the world an image of herself as the only legitimate representative of the Church of Jesus Christ on earth, and of Rome as the nerve-center of world Christianity. Without doubt, however, and in spite of these pretensions, the Orthodox faithful are far more keenly aware than their western brethren that the fullness of the Orthodox Church's witness as a living and dynamic extension of the Incarnation in the world today still continues, completely unaffected by the easy appeal of the "popemobile" and the masses' adulation of the Pope.

Whatever it may be with the Pope's appeal and the adulation of the masses, Orthodoxy has valiantly proven herself still capable of surviving persecution throughout the whole of the twentieth century. Following World War I the massacre of Armenian and Greek Christians by the Turks, and the expulsion of Greeks from cities in Asia Minor such as Ephesus and Smyrna where they were already long established at the time of Christ, was but the beginning.

Almost immediately afterward, Soviet persecution would begin to take full advantage of the twentieth century's technological evolution in persecuting the Church of God. No longer content in confining itself to the traditional sadistic physical torments inflicted on Christians through the centuries, the Soviet Union's highly-trained psychiatrists, physicians and medical workers employed mind-altering drugs and psychological torture to distort, or totally annihilate, the human personality of their victims. How dare anyone believe in God at a time when the government, backed by all the paraphernalia of the latest scientific discoveries (Soviet astronauts had not seen God in space, after all!), decreed there was no God? Individuals believing in God were suspect and a threat to the communist dream of paradise on earth.

Even so, at the end of seven decades of such official, state-supported persecution in the Soviet Union, the demonic powers, acting through the world's most powerful totalitarian regime, and utilizing all the twentieth century's technological sophistication, failed to prevail against the Church of God. Crushed, battered, and left in great disarray, Orthodoxy proved itself more powerful in Russia than all the might of the Soviet Union with its nuclear weapons and space travel. But then had the emerging Church of God in like manner not also survived to triumph at the end of the three centuries of barbarous persecution wielded against her by the equally formidable, and equally God-hating Roman empire, prior to the coming of Constantine the Great?

The on-going witness to this day of Orthodoxy's thousands upon thousands of martyrs and confessors continues to confirm the power of the Holy Spirit at work within the Orthodox Church. Moreover, as post-Soviet times engulf Russia, the hatred and persecution of Orthodoxy there will not cease. It can only continue, whether from without or from within the Church, inspired as such persecution always is, by the Enemy of the human race.

MYSTERY OF THE CHURCH

Yet such internal divisions and demonic struggles continue to reveal to the prayerful soul exactly what the mystery of the Church of God has ever been: a mystery of profound suffering for the truth of who Jesus Christ is. This truth has ever been preserved, proclaimed and made incarnate in the lives of Orthodoxy's faithful as they became participants in His divine sufferings for mankind. They, like the maimed bishops at the Council of Nicea, continue to bear in their bodies *"the marks of the Lord Jesus"* (Gal 6:17).

Orthodoxy survives only to the extent that it continues to be incarnate, since it is not a faith imposed from above by a supreme Pontiff or by some other central authority. By the divine grace of the Holy Spirit, Orthodoxy however cuts a highly visible swathe across two thousand years of history as a mighty *mystical* reality, ever bearing its suffering witness to the historic fact that God was incarnate in Jesus Christ. The holy blood of Orthodoxy's countless martyrs, joined with the unflagging human effort of her faithful, do reveal to those who love God and His Church the presence of the Holy Spirit at work in her today, whatever may be the gross sins of Orthodox people and of their hierarchies.

CHAPTER II

GOD AND HIS CHURCH:
MYSTERIES BEYOND CONCEPTS

Though the perennial image of the Orthodox Church's lack of cohesion is founded on an open, scandalous reality in countries where Orthodoxy has been imported by immigrants, the Orthodox themselves still seem to function serenely with no sign of scandal, be they born Orthodox or converts. In a way inexplicable to outsiders, they seem firmly convinced that the external image of their Church being without any visible cohesion is but an illusion. For them it is obvious that something they call "the" Orthodox Church indeed exists beyond a doubt.

If asked by the outsider how such a strange stance is possible, they might reply that one cannot grasp it without actually becoming a part of the dynamism of that living mystery which is the Church, stretching back across two thousand years of history. Are all Orthodox, living and dead, not indeed united into a simple, vibrant and intimate mystical fellowship? Indeed, for the Orthodox, "the" Orthodox Church is the most basic cosmic reality of their lives, the mystery of its existence informing them both at the deepest and the most exalted levels of their human existence.

To most Western Christians, of course, and more particularly to Roman Catholics, any conception of the Church of God excluding Rome as the spiritual center of world Christianity can only seem suspect. Such a stance not only borders on the scandalous and rebellious, but actually appears blasphemous to them. Quite paradoxically, however, these same Western Christians accept, without question, the incalculable and highly questionable upheavals effected in Western Christianity by Renaissance humanism, as well as its nefarious bicephalous offspring: the Protestant Reformation, and the totalitarian Counter-Reformation. Both efficaciously swept away many now long-forgotten aspects of what the Roman Church actually was in those first thousand years before she abandoned Orthodoxy and Holy Tradition.

The mere fact therefore that the Orthodox Church exists and stands firmly against Roman humanism, having never known either a Reformation or a Counter-Reformation, cannot but be an on-going challenge to the Roman Church's claims for its unique supremacy as the One, Holy, Catholic and Apostolic Church of God in the world. Does the Orthodox Church not demonstrate the full mystery of the Apostolic Church by manifesting the spiritual plenitude of its divine life completely in accord with two thousand years of unbroken Christian tradition? Is that same plenitude not still lived out to the fullest measure within the mystery of the Orthodox Church as she continues to bring forth saints, confessors and martyrs, to say nothing of her constant and unbroken tradition of miracles, wonder-working icons and myrrh-gushing relics?

God's revelation of Himself through the use of matter in the Incarnation of Jesus Christ is continued in Orthodoxy, not only in those living souls united to Him, but also in seemingly "inert matter" that has become holy to God, be it icons or the relics of God's saints. Such wonder-working manifestations exist. In an Orthodox country such as Greece they may even seem commonplace, though unfailingly received by the faithful as highly exceptional graces. To this day myrrh-gushing relics may signal the emergence of new saints. Thus may one conclude that in the Orthodox Church, even as in the time of the Apostles, God's great mercy to the human race does continue to be proclaimed, visibly and tangibly.

As the third millennium of the Christian era dawns, these tangible and visible indications confirm that primitive Christianity not only survives but, through Orthodoxy, is still endowed with its ancient dynamism and wonder-working power. How sharply does such Orthodox witness to primitive Christianity contrast with official Roman attempts to identify the Pope and his followers more and more with the "modern world." One might even discern a strange ploy to convince the masses that the Kingdom of God might be brought to earth, thanks to the Roman Pontiff's unflagging efforts for peace and social justice for all mankind. One is left with the vague impression that over such a regained and earthly paradise the Pope would presumably be expected to preside.

ii

As are so many things we think of as "western," the Rome-centered orientation of western Christian thought is, as we have already observed, essentially provincial in its overview of the Christian reality. A Rome-centered Christianity blithely neglects to take into account the Christian witness offered, for example, by Orthodox Christians in a country such as Greece.

The mystery of the Church of God, as understood by the Orthodox Church, has been lived out in all its plenitude in Greece, with no interruption, since the first century by descendants of the converts of the first apostles, such as St.

17

MYSTERY OF THE CHURCH

Paul. Nor has this unbroken incarnation of the mystery of the Church been accomplished without an unimaginable, and seemingly endless series of incursions, conquests and persecutions, whether by Frankish Crusaders, Turks, Venetians or others, or a combination of all of these.

This is all the more remarkable in that both the Franks and the Venetians were western Christians. In barbaric disdain of the Orthodox as Christian brothers, western crusaders moreover raped and massacred Orthodox Christians, desecrated and pillaged Orthodox churches, and made off with priceless relics. The great accomplishment of the Fourth Crusade in 1204 was the shameful three-day sack of the world's richest center of culture and Christian civilization: Constantinople. Being so disdainfully regarded by rustic, uncouth Crusader knights, the Orthodox people had no choice but to accept that their Christianity must be somehow very different indeed from that of these western barbarians.

The difference between Orthodoxy and western Christianity is, in fact, profound. For example, the Orthodox never question, for "scientific" reasons, the power of God to intervene in His creation when He so wills. Such intervention is not only expected and prayed for by the faithful, but the power of Jesus Christ to intervene and save is still experienced and faithfully pursued throughout Orthodoxy with no apology. Within the Orthodox Church a sense of awe and ineffable sacredness surrounds the mystical action taking place during the Eucharistic Sacrifice. Yet the Orthodox Church feels no need to try to explain, through philosophical terms borrowed from scholasticism, such as Rome's definition of "transubstantiation," just *how* that divine action within this sacred mystery comes about. What is of God is of God and is accepted as such. How could it not be beyond man's concepts?

This is why it seems so natural in Orthodoxy for the apostolic tradition of miracles to live on. This tradition, so evident in the Acts of the Apostles, has been passed down, encouraging, supporting and sustaining the constant, on-going struggle of the Orthodox as they seek to offer Jesus Christ their bodies and souls in a world that hates Him. Whether by the shedding of their blood, or in the more hidden and prolonged martyrdom of serving Him throughout many years of prayer, fasting and suffering self-denial, they all bear witness to the fact that, without exception, every Christian is called to be a "martyr," the Greek word for "witness."

The basic faith of Orthodox Christians is not altogether unlike that of western Christian "fundamentalists," rooted in an unquestioning acceptance of the New Testament and in a profound personal identity with Jesus Christ as Lord and God. In Him, the Incarnation of the Second Person of the Holy Trinity, every pious Orthodox Christian aspires to live and move and have his being. He is therefore worshiped mystically not only as the Bridegroom of the Church, but also personally as the true Bridegroom of every human soul who seeks salvation from the nothingness of death and decay crowning this earthly life, crying out to Him, *"my Lord and my God!"*

It can only follow therefore that the Incarnation of God in Jesus Christ, His virgin birth, and the revelation of God as Father, Son and Holy Spirit are by no means "meaningless dogmas," authoritatively imposed on the Orthodox either from above, or by the past through Holy Tradition. To the contrary, what many contemporary western Christians tend today to view as "out-dated dogmas" are, for the Orthodox, fresh, life-giving tenets. They daily refresh and sustain Orthodox Christians in their own highly personal, interior life in Christ as ever-flowing springs. The dogmas of the Incarnation and of the Holy Trinity provide Orthodox Christians with time-proven means whereby man attempts to partake of the divine, eternal Life of the Divine Bridegroom, Jesus Christ, of Him who said: *"I am the Way, the Truth and the Life"* (Jn 14:6) and *"He that believeth in me, though he were dead, yet shall he live"* (Jn 11:25).

For the Orthodox believer, dogmas are, in the last analysis, simple, historic facts. These facts assure the believer of who he himself is: a creature of God, utterly dependent upon Jesus Christ for salvation from this world of death and decay. They also inform him of who God actually is, as revealed by Jesus Christ: Father, Son and Holy Spirit. It is not without cause that Orthodoxy strikes observant outsiders as being particularly centered on the Holy Trinity. The mystical dynamism of the Holy Trinity at work within her through the Holy Spirit nurtures her Orthodoxy.

Dogmas are therefore never up for negotiation among the Orthodox. The dogma of the Incarnation of God in Jesus Christ, for example, whereby God was revealed as Holy Trinity, and whereby, as St. Athanasius taught, "*God became man that man might become God,*" provides Orthodox man with hope for salvation from the nothingness of his so brief existence on this planet. Touched by the all-saving light of Christ, man's seeming nothingness partakes of God's eternal dynamism and is therefore no longer nothingness.

Through the gift of the Holy Spirit, bestowed out of God's great mercy to him, the Orthodox believer therefore, even though a sinner, knows himself privileged, unworthy as he is, to participate, in the holy and unspeakable mysteries of the eternal Kingdom of the Triune God. The dogmas of the Incarnation and the Holy Trinity allow him to "*taste and see that the Lord is good*" (Ps 34:8), and to experience, in this life, that he is a citizen of the Kingdom of a God whose name is "*Love*" (I Jn 4:8). Encompassed by the mystery of the Church, the heavenly things tasted and partaken of by the pious Orthodox believer can generate within him an ever-deepening longing for greater intimacy with this dynamic God of love. Such a longing can never be satisfied by anything human. To every man's innate loneliness, intimacy with God is the only definitive answer. As illustrated by the great saints, ascetics, martyrs and confessors, this ardent longing for God above all worldly pleasures accords perfectly with what faithful souls have experienced throughout two thousand years of Christian Church history. Orthodox liturgical texts moreover relentlessly challenge the believer to plunge more deeply into this great, mysterious life of the Church that it may become a more dynamic part of his own inner life.

iii

Through pious participation in the unbelievably rich liturgical experiences available in the Orthodox Church, a believer's inner life does inevitably increasingly vibrate with the mystery of the Church. Through a sort of osmosis, liturgical piety more and more shapes his inner life as a Christian. So it is that over a long period of time, the faithful believer not only senses a very personal inner identification with the divine mystery of the Church, but this mystery also becomes for him an ever-burning spiritual presence at work within his heart and soul. How often non-Orthodox observers wonderingly ask why the Orthodox are "the way they are" about their religion: silent, yet impassively unshakeable? This no doubt comes about from the way the Orthodox pray, for each believer's personal prayer is shaped by the time-honored practices of Holy Tradition, a Tradition increasingly not only abandoned by, but, alas! actually forgotten by Rome.

One might cite the example of the Trisagion, or "thrice-holy prayer:" *"Holy God! Holy Mighty! Holy Immortal! Have mercy upon us!"* said to be the prayer of the angels before the face of God. The Trisagion is found at the beginning of all formal Orthodox prayer, public or private, where it leads into the Lord's Prayer. It emphasizes those three characteristic of God not shared by man and which man can acquired only through his life in God: holiness, might and immortality. In the pre-Vatican II Church, this powerful prayer, reduced to a once-a-year status, was sung alternately in Greek and Latin for the veneration of the Cross on Good Friday. How far removed from the oft-repeated daily role it plays in all Orthodox prayer where its implications about the relationship between man and God's holiness, might and immortality resound in accord with Holy Tradition.

Praying both with, and within Holy Tradition allows the believer, encompassed by the mystery of the Church, to realize that he never prays alone. All who have ever prayed for him, all who will ever pray for him, along with unending intercessions of the saints and heavenly powers, constantly surround the Orthodox believer standing before God.

Personal and liturgical prayer, the Sacraments and faithful participation in the fasts and feasts of the Church, all of these serve to sustain the interior life in Christ of the Orthodox believer, enabling him to see well beyond Orthodoxy's sinful divisions. He understands that these divisions do not, in the end, really have anything whatsoever to do with the divine vocation willed for him by God, nor with his potential to pray in the Orthodox Church. His personal vocation as a baptized believer remains intact, whatever befalls. His personal sanctification, through the power of the Holy Spirit, in the One, Holy, Catholic and Apostolic Church of God is the only challenge that matters and that challenge stands before him until his last breath.

Such an Orthodox believer realizes that Orthodox divisions stem either from geographical or historical diversities, or else from trivial, temporal or often quite passing disputes arising between Orthodox groups. They may be ferocious and marked by the unedifying, on-going bitterness and recriminations characterizing family squabbles. Still, those at odds with each other do at times have occasions to recall that their opponents are nonetheless somehow a member of the same family, sharing a mutual identity quite other than the identity shared with heterodox Christians outside the Orthodox faith who may well believe neither in the Holy Trinity nor in the Incarnation of God in Jesus Christ, nor in the virgin birth, and certainly not in Orthodoxy's Holy Tradition of saints, miracles, icons and relics.

This state of affairs contrasts sharply, of course, with western Christian milieux today where political terms such as "right" or "left" may be applied in both Roman Catholic and Protestant milieux, not so much to one's politics, but rather to the degree to which one holds to the very basics of the Catholic or Protestant faith. "Right" and "left" Catholics, as well as "right" or "left" Protestants, may differ on what the tenets of the Christian faith actually are, or on what the essential mission of the Church of God is. Worst of all, they may even differ on just who Jesus Christ is, something totally unimaginable for an Orthodox believer.

iv

Tension and disagreement between Orthodoxy and Roman Christianity over the last thousand years stems largely, it would seem, from lack of spiritual perspective in the West concerning just what the Church is, and where one should seek her. Rome's highly rational over-simplification in associating the Church of God exclusively with the Pope of Rome, above and beyond any other consideration, has meant that a human concept has been substituted for a dynamic mystical reality. Such a substitution inevitably requires endless vain attempts to make the dynamic mystical reality conform to the concept.

This phenomenon was aptly demonstrated by Dostoevsky in his very Orthodox tale of "The Grand Inquisitor" in *The Brothers Karamasov*. There we see how the Inquisitor allowed his own human concept of the Church to be substituted for Christ Himself. Preferring the order and neatness of his own concept, he can only want Christ to disappear and cease challenging Him by His silent presence. Unfortunately, this is by no means limited to Dostoevsky's Grand Inquisitor.

Such a Dostoevskian refutation of Christ is, in fact, easy for any believer who feels he has "arrived" as a Christian and forgets his true position as a creature before Christ, by whom all things were created. It is equally easy once one substitutes some lofty human concept for the living Christ, such as that the Church was founded only on the person of Peter and his successors until the end of time. The mystical reality that the "rock" on which the Church is founded is, in truth, the confession of St. Peter that Jesus Christ is the Son of the Living God, has been usurped. Concept has replaced the living breath of the dynamic Spirit of God, *"present in all places"* and *"filling all things,"* as the Orthodox pray daily. It is much simpler to work with a formula such as "No pope, no Church!" than the dynamism of mystical reality, rooted in the experience of God.

Certainly it is not from lack of devotion to St. Peter that the Orthodox are troubled in regard to the claims of the Pope of Rome. Orthodoxy's devotion to St. Peter is great. She remembers him as the first Bishop of Antioch as well as of Rome and prepares for the Feast of Saints Peter and Paul on June 29 with an accompanying Lent, the only Apostles so honored.

Orthodoxy does have trouble with papal claims, however, when they are in conflict with fidelity to Holy Tradition as it existed for the first thousand years of the Church of God. The abiding truths contained in the Church's first thousand years of experience seem today all but forgotten by the Church of Rome, just as they are also forgotten by her Protestant off-spring.

Yet Rome is not alone in conceptualizing the mystery of the Church. This temptation is ceaselessly proffered believers by the Enemy. The Evil One rightly grasps that the Church of God is the means for the redemption of the race. He would therefore muddy the waters so that all sight of that truth be lost forever and that one view the Church as "just another" religious organization, and Christianity as "just another" religion. All, according to him, is equally valid. He so often tauntingly chides: "That way, isn't man afforded far more choices?"

All such conceptualizations of the ineffable mystery of the Church are therefore really demonic in origin. Even the most faithfully committed Christian who, knowingly, would never question the uniqueness of the role of the Church of Jesus Christ on earth is, nonetheless, never completely free from the demonic temptation to conceptualize. Through such conceptualizations within the mind of even one Orthodox believer, however, the demonic succeeds in infiltrating the very lifeblood of the body of believers, which is the Church. To be delivered from all such betrayals of the great mystery of Christ in His Church, all Orthodox Christians should pray.

v

In rejecting the danger of conceptualizing the mystery of the Church, one is faithfully following the holy Fathers who warn us severely against trying to conceptualize God. They learned, through ascetic experience, that human concepts have their own life, a life rooted in, and nourished by illusions, born of the demonic's subtle mirror-games, flashing ever-changing reflections within man's mind. Though the uncreated Light of Christ should, in principle, shine forth in all its purity through the Church's members into the world, often it seems filtered through human concepts and tainted by the poverty and darkness of man's paltry intellect, vainly trying to cope with God, who is always beyond human intellect. The fire of an encounter with the uncreated Light of the Holy Spirit, however, can completely burn away all need for concepts.

A classic account of such an experience[1] has been left us by a disciple of St. Seraphim of Sarov (1759-1833). During a conversation taking place in a clearing in the forest one winter morning, the author of this account questioned his master:

> *"All the same, I don't understand how one can be certain of being in the Spirit of God. How should I be able to recognize for certain this manifestation in myself?"*

> *"I've already told you," said Father Seraphim, "that it's very simple. I've talked at length about the state of those who are in the Spirit of God; I've also explained to you how we can recognize this presence in ourselves... What more is necessary, my friend?"*
> *"I must understand better everything that you have said to me."*

> *"My friend, we are both at this moment in the Spirit of God... Why won't you look at me?"*

> *"I can't look at you, Father," I replied. "Your eyes shine like lightning; your face has become more*

---

[1] *"Conversation of St. Seraphim on the End of the Christian Life."*

dazzling than the sun, and it hurts my eyes to look at you."

"Don't be afraid," said he, "at this very moment you've become as bright as I have. You are also at present in the fullness of the Spirit of God; otherwise, you wouldn't be able to see me as you do see me."

And leaning towards me, he whispered in my ear, "Thank the Lord God for His infinite goodness towards us. As you've noticed, I haven't even made the sign of the cross; it was quite enough that I had prayed to God in my thoughts, in my heart, saying within myself: 'Lord, make him worthy to see clearly with his bodily eyes, the descent of your Spirit, with which you favour your servants, when you condescend to appear to them in the wonderful radiance of your glory.' And, as you see my friend, the Lord at once granted this prayer of the humble Seraphim... How thankful we ought to be to God for this unspeakable gift which He has granted to us both. Even the Fathers of the Desert did not always have such manifestations of His goodness. The grace of God--like a mother full of loving kindness towards her children--has deigned to comfort your afflicted heart, at the intercessions of the Mother of God herself... Why then, my friend, do you not look me straight in the face? Look freely and without fear; the Lord is with us."

MYSTERY OF THE CHURCH

Encouraged by these words, I looked and was seized by holy fear. Imagine in the middle of the sun, dazzling in the brilliance of its noontide rays, the face of the man who is speaking to you. You can see the movement of his lips, the changing expression of his eyes, you can hear his voice, you can feel his hands holding you by the shoulders, but you can see neither his hands nor his body--nothing except the blaze of light which shines around, lighting up with its brilliance the snow-covered meadow, and the snowflakes which continue to fall unceasingly.

"What do you feel?" asked Father Seraphim.

"An immeasurable well-being," I replied.

"But what sort of well-being? What exactly?"

"I feel," I replied, "such calm, such peace in my soul, that I can find no words to express it."

"My friend, it is the peace our Lord spoke of when he said to his disciples: 'My peace I give unto you,' the peace which the world cannot give; 'the peace which passeth all understanding.' What else do you feel?"

"Infinite joy in my heart."

Father Seraphim continued: "When the Spirit of God descends on a man, and envelops Him in the fullness of His presence, the soul overflows with unspeakable joy, for the Holy Spirit fills everything He touches with joy... If the first-fruits of future joy have already filled your soul with such sweetness, with such happiness, what shall we say of the joy in the Kingdom of Heaven, which awaits all those who weep here on earth. You also, my friend, have wept during your earthly life, but see the joy which our Lord sends to console you here below. For the present we must work, and make continual efforts to gain more and more strength to attain 'the perfect measure of the stature of Christ...' But then this transitory and partial joy which we now feel will be revealed in all its fullness, overwhelming our being with ineffable delights which no one will be able to take from us."

The very need for concepts was burned away and the disciple no longer had questions, but only affirmations. This gift was a very great one.

The wise counsel of the holy Fathers about not trying to conceive of what God is like can serve well also to put us on guard against our perennial temptation to conceptualize the mystery of the Church. Anyone conceptualizing either the mystery of God, or the mystery of God's Church, will inevitably think he no longer needs the protection of the mystery: he has understood everything. He thus ends up choosing darkness rather than the Light since once arrived at a concept, man will seldom abandon it. Indeed, he will find it increasingly necessary to defend *his* concept, clinging to it as he might to his own child. Succeeding concepts will be constructed around it for the purpose of praising it, justifying it and trying to promote it.

The vast body of writings defending the Papacy as a God-inspired institution, first established in the Gospels by our

MYSTERY OF THE CHURCH

Lord Jesus Christ Himself, confirms the truth of this statement. In like manner, so also does the whole library of books defending the "*filioque*" interpolation in the "Creed of Nicea." Such works try to justify what, in reality, was a grave mistake to begin with in altering, however slightly, the original text of the creed arrived at in the first two Ecumenical Councils. Rather than viewing such an alteration as the sin against the mystery of the Church that it was, this unilateral action by Rome has been defended and looked upon as something positive--indeed, a veritable blessing for the human race of which the Orthodox have unfortunately deprived themselves in their pig-headed fidelity to Holy Tradition. Thus has the "*filioque*" been held up not only as a legitimate part of Western Church heritage, but indeed as a "right" to which the Western Church is entitled.

Whatever it may be with the modern Papacy and its betrayal of Holy Tradition, the blatant manifestations of the demonic in this century against God and His Church have been astounding. We have seen men, nations and whole empires twisted and perverted by the powers of darkness. The Lord Himself has promised, however, that the forces of hell, even in the midst of destruction, will not prevail against His Church.

Within the mystery of the Church, the Holy Spirit is always mysteriously at work in the souls of God-fearing Orthodox faithful, as well as in the saints, martyrs and confessors. Rooted in God and in the suffering reality of their flesh and blood, they have, through the Holy Spirit, out of love, and beyond all concepts, nonetheless claimed the Kingdom of the Father, Son and Holy Spirit of Holy Tradition as their own.

31

CHAPTER III

NOT JUST THE "OTHER LUNG"
OF ROMAN CATHOLICISM

After God Himself, the Orthodox Church looks to Holy Scripture and Holy Tradition as the justification of her authority. Her liturgical prayer was already largely in place by the fourth century and, for the most part, has little changed since the eighth century. As she guards the life-giving dogmas of Christianity, her prayer makes evident that Orthodox Christians are distinct and are not to be confused with other Christians. *"Preserve, O God, the holy Orthodox faith and Orthodox Christians until the ages of ages!"* she publicly prays, cutting across all of Orthodoxy's jurisdictional barriers and distinguishing between the Orthodox and the heterodox.

It is prayers such as this that enable the Orthodox faithful to think, as well as speak of "the" Orthodox Church as an identifiable entity, even if not understandable to the heterodox. The outsider, ignorant of this common prayer of all the Orthodox, only sees division. The Orthodox believer, however, grasps that those who pray with him for the salvation of Orthodoxy are, regardless of petty divisions, his true brethren in God.

To the outsider's inquiries, certain Orthodox apologists disconcertingly attempt to speak of the Orthodox Church's fidelity to the Seven Ecumenical Councils and her respect for the famous *"Rudder,"* that remarkable eighteenth century compendium of Orthodox Canon Law by St. Nicodemus the Hagiorite, with all its complexities and, sometimes,

32

contradictions. Such replies, alas! tend to prove of more consolation to the intellectually inclined Orthodox themselves than to the baffled, but sincere, outsider trying to grasp just what Orthodox identity really is. Outsiders often express wonder at what makes Orthodoxy so "spiritual." They are often surprised when one cites fidelity to Holy Tradition and Holy Scripture as the sources for that fullness of Christ they have discovered in Orthodoxy. Reliance on Holy Scripture is familiar enough to them, whereas reliance on Holy Tradition seems almost incomprehensible. As for giving both the same value, that is hard even to conceive for the non-Orthodox.

Until the late fourth century when the canon of the Holy Scriptures was finally fixed by the Church, however, there had of course been nothing but Holy Tradition, maintained by the bishops in communion with one another. Holy Tradition and Holy Tradition alone brought forth the canon of Holy Scriptures. This completely annihilates the Protestant idea of reconstructing the apostolic Church by basing it on Holy Scriptures alone. Thereby is also annihilated the post-schism effort to legitimize papal supremacy based on Holy Scriptures alone, since this supremacy was never a part of Holy Tradition.

ii

Certainly it is the "timelessness" of Orthodoxy that has long set her apart from Western Christianity's evolving manifestations of its heterodox faith. With her unchanging cycle of fasts and feasts, with her remarkably rich liturgical life, she looms on the horizon to sympathetic outsiders as a sort of venerable citadel, a time-honored Christian bastion

33

rising above the sea of change and revisionism today battering Catholics and Protestants as never before. As both awkwardly attempt to staunch the hemorrhage of European dechristianization, their efforts to prove themselves "meaningful" and "relevant" to "modern man" prove discouragingly impotent.

On the other hand, Orthodoxy's tenacious fidelity to Holy Tradition with its basic, apostolic Christianity, has won for her, from no one less than the Pope of Rome the title of "the other lung" of the Roman Catholic Church. Certain Orthodox, having lost sight of their own Orthodoxy, have even been flattered by this papal metaphor.

The metaphor is misplaced if it wishes to imply that Orthodoxy is lacking a lung. Within the mystery of the Church of God, as lived out by the Orthodox, no lung has ever been lacking, for Orthodoxy experiences no difficulty in breathing. The breath of the Holy Spirit has unfailingly formed, for two thousand years, those martyrs, saints and confessors whereby the glory of the Incarnation of Jesus Christ continues in the world.

Or is the Pope implying that the Roman Church is experiencing difficulty in breathing and that perhaps it is a "lung," or some other vital part which is not functioning properly in the Rome's own organism? If that be the case, then the Pope himself has recognized what the Orthodox have long known to be a serious problem in the modern Roman Church.

Can Rome seriously think that her vitally "missing lung" might painlessly be reclaimed, and her health immediately improved by such a massive, painless graft of Orthodoxy onto her Catholic organism? Such a solution could not even begin to touch the problem Rome has created for herself through her arrogantly unilateral evolution over the past thousand years as she proudly assumed herself to be the whole of the One, Holy, Catholic and Apostolic Church of God. In any case, the papal metaphor suggests that Rome somehow assumes that as "mother church" it would suffice for her to open wide her maternal arms, and welcome into their embrace a submissive Orthodox Church, with no questions asked on either side. Even to entertain such thoughts speaks of an abysmal lack of understanding of what Orthodoxy really is.

Orthodoxy cannot but lament the sin of the Roman Church's separation from her. She grasps quite easily that once Rome had abandoned Orthodox Holy Tradition for unilateral evolution, something vital to Rome's continuing as an authentic Orthodox part of the Church of God, and bearing common witness with her four ancient sister Patriarchates, was bound to be lost.

However much the Orthodox Church may prayerfully grieve over the Roman Church's abandoning that Holy Tradition that once united them, she also must recognize that Rome did thereby sin against the mystery of the Church as she embarked on her unilateral experiment by proclaiming herself supreme. At the end of the twentieth century it has moreover become increasingly evident how unfortunate Rome's experiment with Renaissance humanism has proven. Today her own innate Protestant sectarianism becomes more blatantly manifest in all she does.

Certainly the papal metaphor affords an unwitting revelation of the Pope's deep concerns about the present state of health of the Church of Rome. Yet surely the Pope must be aware that it was only in 1870, as heaven raged, and as lightening crashed around St. Peter's, that the Pope of Rome was dramatically proclaimed, at the first Vatican Council, the supreme and infallible head of the one true Church of God.

What is obvious is that the papal metaphor, supposedly so flattering for the Orthodox, fails to show any grasp of the basic, vital necessity for Rome to descend from her self-elevated pinnacle of universal primacy to join, just as she once did, in charity, mutual love and true unity of faith and dogma with the ancient patriarchates of Jerusalem, Antioch, Alexandria and Constantinople. How could those four ancient patriarchates, as also the faithful in communion with them, take Rome's self-proclaimed papal dogma of 1870 seriously when this was never a part of that Holy Tradition they have guarded uninterruptedly for two thousand years as Orthodox Christians? If the Roman Church is experiencing difficulty in breathing today, is the Orthodox position not thereby given greater credence? Rome's difficulties can only stem from her having arrogantly struck out on her own and, in so doing, abandoning Holy Tradition by proclaiming herself supreme over all.

As the "eastern rite churches" have painfully learned, Rome always believes herself superior to Holy Tradition since she believes she is herself that Holy Tradition. She therefore must set the tone for the conduct for all "eastern rite churches," even if this contradicts matters pertaining to that Holy Tradition of Orthodoxy to which they try to cling. That basic problem has never really been satisfactorily resolved by Rome and, indeed, cannot be resolved. The Orthodox instinct of the "eastern rite churches" for the absolute sacredness of Holy Tradition is never felt more keenly than when they attempt to embrace the sectarian orientation of the Roman Catholic Church as she has existed since the Council of Trent. Caught between two fires, the "eastern rite churches" find that the trappings of papal supremacy go against their own Orthodox instincts since they contradict Orthodoxy's Holy Tradition.

In the twentieth century alone, Rome's record in guarding her formerly sacred western Christian traditions has proven appalling. To mention only the two most obvious, that is the pre-Communion fast, and Friday abstinence from meat, these universal traditions were abandoned with light heart, from one day to the next, in the wake of Vatican II. This is, of course, a tribute to the efficiency of a totalitarian regime provided by papal supremacy.

Such an efficiency has often tempted many Orthodox but, by the grace of God, has never been possible to bring about without violating the sacred mystery of the Church. Thanks to the corrective nature of having four sister Patriarchates, the maintenance of Holy Tradition going back to the Apostles is never entrusted to one Patriarch alone.

Rome increasingly confounded Holy Tradition with the office of the Pope so that one, single office came to be regarded as the only really absolute "tradition" mattering in this world or the next. With the rise of the Papacy, all sense of the absolutely sacred character of Holy Tradition got lost and Holy Tradition's indispensable role in the mystery of the Church largely disappeared from the whole of western Christendom.

MYSTERY OF THE CHURCH

The Roman Church, if she really wishes to become Orthodox again, must rediscover the essential holiness of Holy Tradition apart from the Pope. This can never be done easily, however, simply by patronizingly opening her arms to the Orthodox with no questions asked. Rather must she humbly seek to rediscover the essential holiness of Holy Tradition within the mystery of the Church as it still may be found, latent and dormant, in her own past, and come to cherish that holiness of the past so that it informs her present life in Christ.

Rome has repeatedly demonstrated arrogance towards the Orthodox and, even when she would appear well-disposed, seldom goes beyond a patronizing attitude. This, of course, frees her from any compulsion to look on the Orthodox Church as a really equal church and not regard it as just an ethnic curiosity, or a series of charming provincial museum pieces left behind in Christian history which she, Rome, by divine grace, is ordained to correct. In trying to enforce clerical celibacy on certain of her eastern rite clergy, for example, Rome disregarded completely the unbroken Christian tradition for married priests from the beginning of the Church of God. What better confirmation is needed to prove that, in the average Catholic mind, married Orthodox priests can only be regarded as inferior, undisciplined and second-rate?

As for the Orthodox Church, in all her many crushing humiliations she has always known herself to be, by the grace of God, the One, Holy, Catholic and Apostolic Church of Christ, whatever adversities befall her.

MYSTERY OF THE CHURCH

iii

Exactly as Protestants became sectarian in separating from the main stream of Western Christianity in the sixteenth century, so also has the Roman Church increasingly become sectarian as she exercised her unilateral freedom with no concern whatsoever for what her sister Patriarchates might have to say. The totalitarian qualities inherent in the office of the Papacy have made this possible. Radical changes have thus been effected which, like the Protestant Reformation, have profoundly altered her memory of the past. This has inevitably resulted in the Roman Church's ever becoming more sectarian than before, just as the Protestants also continue to prove themselves more sectarian. Still, both think Orthodoxy has nothing whatsoever to do with them or with what they are as Christians.

Tenaciously, Rome still clings to her position of viewing the Pope of Rome not just as the successor of St. Peter but makes of him the supreme world arbitrator in spiritual matters, that is, *"Christ's vicar on earth,"* with universal authority over all members of the One, Holy, Catholic and Apostolic Church of God. This highly sectarian position, as presented today, was unknown for the first thousand years of Christian history. Yet Rome clings to it as it were with a death grip, staking her whole identity upon it.

For the Orthodox, the Roman Church's position in regard to papal authority not only means that Holy Tradition has been confounded with the too-earthly office of the Pope of Rome, but that in Roman eyes, should the Pope of Rome so will, Holy Tradition, as seen and preserved by the Orthodox, can always be changed instantly or overthrown with no reference whatsoever either to the past or the other four Patriarchates. So has it come about that, not being answerable to anyone else, the Pope became, in Catholic eyes, the one sure mark of Holy Tradition.

Fidelity to papal teaching, the much-lauded talisman of the *"magisterium of the Church"* really means the *"magisterium of the present Pope."* It is the one distinguishing feature prevailing today as orthodoxy in the Roman Church, regardless of what might be the unbroken Christian tradition of the four sister Patriarchates of Antioch, Alexandria, Jerusalem and Constantinople. For example, in regard to the question of required celibacy for priests of the Church of God, it is the Pope's stand, not that of Holy Tradition, that must prevail for a Catholic of good faith. Doubts cast upon Rome's stance by the historical witness and unbroken tradition of the Orthodox Church are definitely not appreciated in Catholic circles, however justified they may be.

As for unbroken tradition, a very simple example suffices to point out this basic divergence with Roman Catholicism. St. Basil the Great and St. John Chrysostom, both born in the fourth century and authors of the Orthodox Church's two major liturgies, are today separated from us by more than a millennium and a half. They would, however, feel far less disoriented with what goes on in the Sunday worship of an Orthodox parish in North America today than would some mere seventy year-old Catholic, born in the twentieth century, and strictly reared in the pre-Vatican II Church. After a hiatus of a mere forty years, such a Catholic, if suddenly finding himself in a Sunday Mass in his old parish today, would, with horror and no small sense of curiosity, instinctively recoil from what he saw taking place there as the worship of some heretofore unknown Protestant sect.

First with the Council of Trent, and again with Vatican I and Vatican II, Roman Catholicism has openly--and, as it were, with a vengeance--repeatedly confirmed her own latent Protestantism. Things both new and novel have not only been introduced, but, thanks to the totalitarian nature of papal supremacy, have also been enforced upon the whole of the Roman Church's fabric at every level, whether regarding her liturgical life or her religious life. Much as was done by the Protestants who broke with the Catholic tradition of their times in the name of free interpretation of the Holy Scriptures, once the Roman Church confounded Holy Tradition with the office of the Pope of Rome, all checks and balances were removed, and Rome had no sister Patriarchate to answer to for her unilateral and arbitrary actions.

The Orthodox, patiently clinging to Apostolic traditions, therefore reject categorically that heresy by which the Roman Catholic faithful are identifiable, that is that the Pope is *"Christ's vicar on earth,"* and the supreme and infallible head of the Church of God. Enamored with the office of the Pope to the extent of confounding that office with Holy Tradition itself, the Roman Church has ended up not only by eliminating Holy Tradition's fullness, but also by turning her back on Holy Tradition's complexities and basic inconveniences. These, of course, still challenge the Orthodox as they strive to live as Christians in today's modern, pragmatic world. It is a world interested only in statistics and efficiency, a world where miracles and the great wonders of God are scorned and mocked as contemptible

41

fodder, fit only for the gullible and illiterate. Having found themselves free to pass over, disregard, set aside, change and eventually even totally forget any tradition not of particular interest to them, the incumbents of St. Peter's throne have left the West with a church that would be unrecognizable to one of their predecessors of a thousand years ago. Once the other four Patriarchates could be dismissed as "schismatics," the image of apostolic Christianity being revealed in the communion of the Patriarchates with one another in humility and love was no longer needed. Rome was very far from her present need--if we are to believe the Pope--for a "second lung." The Papacy, and the Papacy alone sufficed.

Orthodoxy still nonetheless recognizes the Pope of Rome as the Patriarch of the West, even though, in seeking to bolster his claim of universal jurisdiction, he led his faithful into abandoning Orthodoxy. Moreover, the fact that Orthodoxy has never set up a rival Patriarchate in Rome serves to underline Orthodoxy's historical recognition of Rome by her patriarchates, completely in accord with Holy Tradition. This tradition was violated by Rome, however, in her arrogant military and ecclesiastical forays into Orthodox territory during the Crusades and still, to this day, is blatantly evident in a place such as Jerusalem.

Were the Pope to return to Orthodoxy he would certainly once more be in communion with his four brother patriarchs, and partake of the same chalice. This does not alter the fact that as honored as the Pope might have been at the time of the councils as representing the successor of St. Peter, first of the Apostles, Orthodoxy remembers that he was always very far from being, in the minds of the holy fathers assembled there, that isolated "supreme Pontiff" he has become today by a unilateral and highly contested decision made only in 1870.

Orthodoxy has proven, through her two thousand years of experience, the pragmatic fact that the mystery of the Church is not, nor has it ever been, a *temporal* mystery concerned with "the Church militant" as understood and preached by Rome. Rather is it a *spiritual* mystery, the timeless mystery of the Church understood as the suffering Bride of the suffering Bridegroom, flagellated, crowned with thorns and spat upon.

Orthodoxy knows that Holy Tradition can never be tied to any one prelate's temporal limitations, be he the Pope of Rome or the Patriarch of Jerusalem. Having lived out the experience of the mystery of the Church for two thousand years, the Orthodox Church, as the living, mystical Bride of the suffering Christ, experiences a great freedom in the Holy Spirit. She does not feel the need to seek, claim, proclaim or impose spiritual and mystical unity in Christ by passing through the temporal power of a "Supreme Pontiff" with all the hype and glitter of the personality cult surrounding him. Orthodoxy's burning life in Christ Himself allows her, through the Holy Spirit, to experience the fullness of truth that streams from Orthodoxy's partaking, from the same chalice, of Him Who is the life-giving Bread of Life. A tangible, mystical unity is thus maintained in her faithful by the Holy Spirit, by Him Who never ceases to act in her to the greater glory of the Father.

Though holiness, since it is of God, generally remains inconceivable and incomprehensible for the human mind, it is nonetheless a mystery experienced by Orthodox Christians.

MYSTERY OF THE CHURCH

It is a truth born from the Orthodox believer's life in Christ as he strives, day after day, to live out the mystery of holiness in the fallen world. Yet he can never explain it, any more than he can explain the mystery of life itself.

In the profoundest sense possible, of course, Orthodoxy is life itself, mortal, human life as it is known to every man. Yet it is also that life already in the process of being transfigured, in the here and now, by Him who said, "*I am come that they might have life, and that they might have it more abundantly*" (Jn 10:10). By the grace of God revealed in the Orthodox Church, eternal life in Jesus Christ can still be experienced and communicated today to Orthodox Christians through God's great mercy to her. It is a life which, through the Holy Spirit, and within the Orthodox Church, affords, already in this fallen world, a vibrant foretaste of heaven to every man who seeks God.

The vocation of the Orthodox Church is to keep this possibility of tasting heaven on earth available to all who seek to be saved from the limits of their own mortality. Within the mystery of the Church of God, as understood by the Orthodox, such salvation remains an ever-beckoning possibility to every soul who, in humility, seeks salvation and approaches the mystery of the Orthodox Church with fear of God, with faith and with love.

CHAPTER IV

THE HEART OF THE MYSTERY:
THE KINGDOM OF A TRIUNE GOD

Non-Orthodox Christians never fail to be struck by the implacable number of references to the Holy Trinity in Orthodox worship. There the glorification of the Father, Son and Holy Spirit is something far more than the familiar Trinitarian formula recited after the psalms and common both to Eastern and Western churches. References to the triune God not only begin and end all Orthodox actions, but permeate all liturgical texts. Far more than either Catholics or Protestants, the Orthodox emphasize not only that God is always triune in nature, but that the religion of Jesus Christ, properly expressed, inevitably leads one back, at every possible moment, and in all possible circumstances, to the Father, Son and Holy Spirit.

Orthodoxy is equally keen in referring to the dual nature of Jesus Christ the *"only-begotten Son and Word of God,"* as one sings at the Divine Liturgy. Orthodoxy glories in the words of St. John the Theologian: *"And the Word made flesh and dwelt among us, (and we beheld his glory, the glory as of the only begotten of the Father) full of grace and truth"* (Jn 1:14).

By beginning his Gospel with the words: "*In the beginning was the Word, and the Word was with God, and the Word was God,"(Jn 1:1)* St. John immediately implies the Trinity in introducing and defining the Word, the Trinity's Second Person. Made flesh in Jesus Christ, the Word had, in fact, existed from the beginning with God and was the Creator of all things: "*All things were made by him, and without him was not anything made that was made*" (Jn 1:3). Since, in Orthodoxy, "theology" can only refer to matters pertaining to the Holy Trinity, one understands why John the Evangelist is usually referred to by the Orthodox as "John the Theologian."

At the very heart of the Orthodox faith reside two basic and fundamental theological mysteries, the "*true knowledge*" of which constitutes "*true Orthodoxy*," according to St. Gregory of Sinai. The first mystery is of the one God in three Persons: Father, Son and Holy Spirit; the second that of the two natures--human and divine--of Jesus Christ who, without any confusion, is both perfect God and perfect man.

"*True knowledge*" implies more, of course, than mere intellectual assent to the possibility that these two mysteries might be true. One arrives at "true knowledge" from an on-going spiritual effort to inform and enlighten one's inner-most life by the truths contained in the seemingly irreconcilable and contradictory formula: True Orthodoxy is the sum of (3 = 1) plus (2 = 1).

The faithful Orthodox soul strives to fuse the two elements of this equation not only one with the other, but also with the basic mystery of his own personal, inner life in God since even the way he signs the cross bears witness to this fusion, as also to his personal allegiance to it. The thumb and first two fingers are joined together, signifying the triune nature of God as Trinity, while the two remaining fingers, bent down on the hand, represent the two natures of Christ: human and divine.

This fusion is even more dramatically expressed whenever an Orthodox bishop gives his blessing during

46

liturgical worship. In one hand he bears the *trikiri*, or holder for three candles, positioned so as to join in one flame; in the other hand he bears the *dikiri*, holding two candles, also positioned to make one flame. When the blessing is given the bishop raises his hands with a candle holder in each, then crosses his arms. The double mystery of the Holy Trinity and of the dual nature of Christ in one Person is thus proclaimed without confusion or vagueness concerning the distinctiveness of the two and the three. In the inextricable, mysterious relationship of these two mysteries the Orthodox Church rejoices while maintaining a remarkable balance deep within herself. In what might be called a cyclical or circular movement, the revelation of the Holy Trinity through the Incarnation of the Son causes the believer, fixed on Him, to move unfailingly back to the three Persons in One God from whence the Incarnation sprang. The two are inextricably joined.

Non-Orthodox Christians never cease to be astounded on discovering that the Gospel read on Easter night at the Divine Liturgy of Pascha--in some Slavic parishes even declaimed in a number of languages to emphasize its universality--is never an account of the scene at the tomb. Rather is it the Prologue to St. John's Gospel proclaiming the identity of Him who arose for the dead: *"In the beginning was the Word, and the Word was with God, and the Word was God"* (Jn 1:1).

Prior to the Paschal Liturgy, of course, the Gospel of the myrrh-bearing women's discovery at the tomb has already been proclaimed during the outdoor Resurrection ceremonies immediately preceding Pascal Matins. The first barrage of *"Christ is risen!"* *"Indeed He's risen!"* with the accompanying exchanges of the kiss of Easter by the faithful has also already joyfully burst forth and the Easter hymn (troparion), *"Christ is risen from the dead having trampled down death by death, and upon those in the tombs having life bestowed!"* interminably repeated. Prior to arriving at the solemn moment for the Gospel, both throughout Paschal Matins and during the first part of the Paschal Liturgy, exchanges of *"Christ is risen!" "Indeed He's risen!"* have also relentlessly continued to erupt every time the priest censes the faithful.

Finally, having arrived at that solemn moment when Orthodoxy is perhaps more herself than at any other time of the year, the focus is suddenly shifted to the theological identity of that crucified One who was raised from the dead: Jesus Christ, in Whom was incarnate the Word of God and Second Person of the Holy Trinity. Thus on the night of Pascha, and at the high feast of the Lamb, Orthodoxy stoutly reaffirms her two basic mysteries: the two natures of Christ through which God was revealed as Holy Trinity.

The triune nature of God and the two natures of Christ are intimately related not only to the way Orthodox Christians bear witness to their holy Orthodox faith, but also to how they pray. For example, the twelve-word Jesus Prayer, lying at the heart of Orthodox ascetical aspirations of monastics and others to *"pray without ceasing"* (I Thess 5:17), is profoundly Trinitarian when understood in its Orthodox context. Commonly referred to as "the prayer" among monastics, it is not at all just some sort of eastern Christian practice based on the employment of mantras as in Hinduism and Buddhism. Indeed, its twelve words, *"Lord Jesus Christ, Son of God, have mercy upon me, a sinner,"* require the uniquely Christian confession of Jesus as "Lord," something *"that no man can say [...] but by the Holy Spirit"* (I Cor

48

12:3), according to St. Paul. Thus, each time the believer repeats this most-repeated of all prayers in Orthodoxy, the Holy Spirit is confessing, through him who prays it, the Lordship of Jesus Christ to the greater glory of God the Father. In a mystical sense he who prays "the prayer" becomes a living temple of the Holy Spirit who, in him, is repeatedly confessing the Holy Trinity.

ii

The Orthodox Church is keenly aware of her divine mission as representative of the Kingdom of the Holy Trinity in the world, knowing she is the One, Holy Catholic and Apostolic Church of God on earth and hence responsible for the salvation of the human race. Whatever deficiencies exist in her witness because of the many sins of her own people, Orthodoxy does, in her worship, faithfully point all mankind to the Uncreated Light of the Risen Christ, to Him through whom the Holy Trinity was first revealed to the world. An outpost in this world of the Kingdom of the Father, Son and Holy Spirit, one God, she, through Him, continues to draw men to Him, "*the only lover of mankind*," as one hears so oft repeated in Orthodox prayers and hymns.

For almost two millennia Orthodoxy has never wavered in associating herself with this divine mission and boldly proclaims it at the beginning of every Divine Liturgy. The first words of the priest-celebrant audible to the faithful are a bold proclamation of this fact. Facing the altar and raising the Gospel-book before God for all to see, the priest intones solemnly: "*Blessed is the Kingdom of the Father, Son and Holy Spirit!*" to which a firm "*Amen!*" is sung in answer, leading the faithful once again into the Divine Liturgy's first Litany of supplications for the Orthodox and for the whole world.

By raising the Gospel-book containing the historical accounts of the coming into the world of Jesus Christ at the time of Caesar Augustus, the priest fuses historical time with the eternity of God's Kingdom of the Holy Trinity. This short proclamation also summons believers to draw nigh with open hearts and love of God to partake of what is about to be manifest through the celebration of the Holy Mysteries of the Christian altar: the power and life of the Holy Trinity made available and tangible to man through the mystical sacrifice of Jesus Christ.

This initial exclamation beginning the Divine Liturgy usually prompts a silent ripple of recognition from the congregation. Certain of the faithful may make a prostration, face bowed to the floor. Others may simply cross themselves and touch the floor with their right hand. Almost all, however, if by nothing but a simple bow and a sign of the cross, will somehow signal that they are aware that the Divine Liturgy is beginning.

By whatever sign of devotion they choose, the faithful thereby confirm their own personal tie with that Kingdom of the Father, Son and Holy Spirit, now about to take on, through the mystery of the Church, the visible and tangible dimensions given it on earth in Orthodoxy. The Holy Gifts of bread and wine, already prepared, will, in the course of the Eucharistic Sacrifice now beginning, solemnly be set forth on the altar and consecrated as the Body and Blood of Jesus Christ.

MYSTERY OF THE CHURCH

These various signs of recognition, assent, and reverent awe of the faithful are, of course, merely outward expressions of the deep and inner grace of the Holy Spirit spiritually at work in their midst. By them the believer expresses his own personal, humble assent, in the here and now, to what is about to take place not only in that church, but in all Orthodox churches where the Divine Liturgy is celebrated. The victory of Christ won by His Passion, Death, Burial, Resurrection and Ascension is a cosmic one. Liturgically therefore one is able to join oneself to it unconditionally, beyond all time or space. The beginning of the Divine Liturgy is also the believer's personal invitation to turn aside from worldly preoccupations and partake of that eternal Kingdom revealed by, and still to be found in, Jesus Christ alone. This invitation is more specifically renewed in mid-Liturgy in the Cherubic Hymn: *"Let us lay aside all earthly care that we may receive the King of all."*

iii

The "other worldly" dimension of Orthodox worship does bear strong witness to Orthodoxy's authenticity as the One, Holy, Catholic and Apostolic Church of God on earth. It was because Orthodox worship conveyed such an overwhelming sense of actually bringing heaven down to earth that the emissaries of Prince Vladimir of Kiev, in the X. century, recommended that the prince opt for Orthodoxy as the religion of his people. In some mysterious and inexplicable way during Orthodox worship in Hagia Sophia in Constantinople, they had felt unsure of whether they were still on earth or already in heaven, something they had not experienced in Rome.

The on-going experience of tasting heaven on earth nurtures the Orthodox faithful and is present whenever they think with piety on the mystery of the Church. They know from experience that she is indeed the depository of the fullness of Christ and of the Kingdom of heaven. As the earthly outpost of the Kingdom of the Holy Trinity, the Church claims their allegiance as subjects of that eternal Kingdom untouched by time. It is a Kingdom to which they have recourse in all their earthly needs and after which they still aspire with their last breath.

As the Orthodox Church summons all men to return to the eternal Kingdom of the Father, Son and Holy Spirit, her voice is of particular appeal to those who have "*put on Christ*" in baptism. Orthodox baptism is particularly enlightening in this respect.

The candidate is turned to face the West and thrice called upon to renounce the Prince of this world and, each time, to breathe and spit on him. The candidate is next turned to face the East and asked, again three times, if he accepts Christ and, each time, told to bow before Him. The dichotomy between the kingdom of this world, of which Satan is Prince, and the kingdom of the Father, Son and Holy Spirit into which, through his baptism into Christ, the new believer is now being mystically introduced, is thus sharply emphasized.

Having opted for the uncreated Light of Christ over the darkness of this world, and having himself been made resplendent with the Light of the Holy Trinity, the baptized believer, in a mystical sense, has, from that moment, become a stranger to this world, even while living in it. Whenever he remembers his baptism, he can never again feel fully at home in this world. Has he not thrice renounced, and thrice spat upon, the Prince of this world? Has he not opted to become a citizen of the kingdom of the Holy Trinity by bowing down three times before Christ? Although the eternal kingdom of the Father, Son and Holy Spirit will be enjoyed unimpeded only beyond this lifetime, where death and decay await all who breathe, the life-giving kingdom of Christ has, even now, already been made accessible to him who is willing to seek God with fear, faith and love.

The most immediate goal for the baptized believer, however, is not that of merely avoiding eternal death through the promise of eternal life accorded believers in Christ--as it were "pie in the sky." It is far more immediate and firmly rooted in the here and now. The sanctification of his whole being through an ever-increasing participation in the mysteries of the divine kingdom is his goal. By the power of the Holy Spirit and an ever-deepening indwelling of Christ in him, and through liturgical and personal prayer, he will increasingly draw nearer to the holiness of life in the eternal Kingdom where all the patriarchs, prophets, forefathers, saints, confessors and martyrs made perfect in faith have gone before.

Participation in the mysteries and offices celebrated in the Orthodox Church thus allows sinful, fallen man to make a start in reclaiming the kingdom of the Holy Trinity and its glory for his own. Ever compassionate, the Orthodox Church knows that the on-going, life-long attempt of fallen, prodigal sons and daughters to pull away from the kingdom of this world and return to the eternal kingdom of the Holy Trinity can never be easy. Man, in spite of his best intentions, usually finds himself attempting to make himself "at home" in this fallen world, as if it were his final destination. A faithful believer, however, identifying himself with the Prodigal Son, finds himself rising up, again and again, turning his back on the totally unsatisfactory swine's trough of "normal" life to return to the heavenly Father.

It is exactly such an on-going and repeated act of return that is implied when the Orthodox Church prays that *"we may spend the rest of our lives in peace and repentance."* Unfortunately the word "repentance," given its English associations, fails completely to convey the joy of the thought of leaving the swineherd to return to the sweet fragrance of the Father's house. Orthodoxy understands that joy, however, and therefore prays fervently and regularly that all her prodigal sons and daughters may persevere in rising up again and again to return to the kingdom into which they gained citizenship by baptism.

In spite of being both guardian and dispenser of the kingdom of the Holy Trinity, the Orthodox Church nonetheless still never claims that entrance into that kingdom is denied anyone outside her fold. Only God holds the key to such great, eternal and divine secrets. Only God knows the outcome of His own divine economy. Since it is a mystery beyond her knowledge, the Orthodox Church therefore can only bow prayerfully before the words of her Lord: *"Other sheep I have, which are not of this fold: them also I must bring"* (Jn 10:16).

Indeed, the Orthodox Church does not set herself up as a supreme and unique earthly power divinely endowed as the ultimate in legitimizing human custom. Nor does she hold herself to be an authority who puts a stamp of divine approval on the social mores of any given ethnic society. Rather, the Orthodox Church is a world-wide beacon, beaming forth the glory of the Holy Trinity upon the whole human race, challenging it in all its various activities, to return to the Kingdom of the triune God from which it fell in Adam.

iv

The Kingdom of the Holy Trinity is, in fact, within the mystery of the church, the only Kingdom the Church is allowed to claim as her own. This is a great truth unfortunately neglected by Orthodoxy's sister Church of Rome. With Rome's pressing desire to be first and the one true head of the spiritual Kingdom of Christ on earth, she forgets that what is of the earth is earthly, and what is of heaven is heavenly. Therefore, the extent to which she attempts to claim for herself an earthly kingdom, is the same extent to which, unwittingly but inevitably, she, divorces herself from her divine Bridegroom.

Within the mystery of the Church His kingdom is, as He reminded Pilate, *"not of this world"* (Jn 18:36). The Pope's claims of world supremacy, culminating in 1870 in the dogma of infallibility, a dogma espoused and expostulated by Rome to this day, are both totally foreign to Orthodox's Holy Tradition, as we have seen.

The key to Orthodoxy's richness and diversity, as well as to her inextricable fusion with apostolic Christianity, is above all discernable in her deep regard for Holy Tradition, a regard equaled only by her regard for the Holy Scriptures. Indeed, separation from Holy Tradition can only lead to something sectarian, something no longer recognizable to those who have gone before.

Orthodoxy's fidelity to the past accounts for the strange distance so keenly felt whenever a westerner tries to grasp Orthodox worship. It also explains why, for the Orthodox, western worship often seems so thin, so cold, and so lacking in the ineffable glory of God. Even God Himself somehow seems cold, formal and distant in western worship, in spite of magnificent choirs and organs, and choral masses sung with orchestras and opera stars. The glory of intimate prayer, of tearful communion of believers with God Himself, such basic and very Christian aspirations are seldom to be experienced in such elaborate and artistically charged settings.

Whatever the merit of so-called "charismatic" worship, those noisy "manifestations of the Spirit," like that of special masses featuring rock bands, guitars, folk music, drums and dancing processions, inevitably show a certain lack of seriousness with their child-like unbridling of very human passions. When one stands before Almighty God should that normal solemnity demanded in the courts of flawed human justice suddenly crumble? Holy Tradition encourages man, in all his inadequacy, to bow low before the face of God in respectful, awed silence when he is invited to the mystic wedding supper of the Lamb, and certainly before he, a sinner, presumes to partake of His Holy Table.

Having opted for the kingdom of this world in wanting to impose upon it their own ideas for establishing a Christian regime, both the Roman and the Protestant Churches have lost sight of the very heart of the mystery of the Church: the Kingdom of the Father, Son and Holy Spirit is the only kingdom the Bride of Christ can ever claim as her own.

MYSTERY OF THE CHURCH

Outside that kingdom, the Church languishes and inevitably takes on the characteristics of the world, finding herself increasingly submitted to the machinations of the Prince of this world. Thus is explained the general confusion among western Christians today regarding what the Church is and where it is to be found.

For the Church of God is ever the Bride of the Immolated Bridegroom, Jesus Christ, "*the head of the body, the church,*" (Col 1:18) as the Apostle wrote to the Colossians. The Bride of such a Bridegroom can never glory either in herself or in the glory of this world. Only in the glory that He, the crucified One, had with the Father "*before the world was*" (Jn 17:5) does she glory. This is the glory of the Holy Trinity, to be sure, made even more glorious for believers by the vision of the Lamb, "*slain from the foundation of the world,*" (Rev 13:8) the Son of the Virgin, the Church's Bridegroom, "*a deified man, yet marked with wounds.*"

CHAPTER V

THE MYSTERY'S LEGACY: "RIGHT GLORY"

When Saints Cyril and Methodius, brothers from Thessaloniki, undertook the evangelization of the neighboring Slavs in the mid-ninth century, they translated the Greek word "orthodox" into Slavonic by two words: "right glory." Thanks to this early ninth century translation, the mystical and theological meaning of the word "orthodox" has been preserved and clarified. Slavic Orthodox Christians, be they Bulgarian, Russian, Serbian or Ukrainian, proudly remind the world that they are "right glory" Christians and belong to the "right glory" church.

When contrasted with the word "heterodox," meaning "other glory," a term generally applied by the Orthodox to non-orthodox Christians, the felicity of this translation is immediately elucidated. Indeed, at the root of both words lies "doxa," the Greek word for "glory," justifying the translation both of "orthodox" as "right glory," and of "heterodox" as "other glory." Enshrined forever in the texts of the Slavonic Churches as the real meaning of "orthodox," the concept of "right glory" has thus not been lost. Its profound implications are still very much alive to challenge all Orthodox Christians, be they Greek, Slav or North American.

It is of course curious that today's Greek-speakers are usually surprised as much as are non-Orthodox Christians when they see "orthodox" translated by "right glory." Even a Greek who has been exposed to his Slavic brethren and their Orthodoxy may stolidly maintain that "orthodox" in Greek can really only mean either "right teaching," "right thinking," "right speaking," or, in the church context, "right doctrine." Never, he usually maintains, can it mean "right glory" in Greek.

Obviously a certain evolution in the understanding of the meaning of the Greek word "orthodox" has taken place among Greek-speakers since the early ninth century. Certainly one can hardly put in doubt either the Orthodoxy or the linguistic competence of Saints Cyril and Methodis, two high-born Greek-speaking missionary brothers and monks of Thessaloniki, of superior education in both the "earthly" and the "angelic" sciences.

"Right glory" is a term particularly helpful for English-speakers when trying to understand "Orthodoxy." When they hear a Greek trying to convey what the great and wondrous mystery of his Church is, how much easier it would be if only the Greek himself could use the words, "right glory"! One's debt to the Slavic churches for preserving, over the past thousand years, the spiritual understanding of what "orthodox" meant to Saints Cyril and Methodius is therefore inestimable.

The paradox of the Greeks having forgotten that "orthodox" once meant "right glory" is not only curious, but surprising theologically. It is, in fact, the "glory"--"doxa"--of God that inextricably fuses the revelation of God in the Old Testament with the revelation of Jesus Christ in the New Testament. Did the glory surrounding the Son's coming into the world not provide a sign to those who loved the God of Abraham, Isaac and Jacob that there was indeed a genuine continuity with that awesome and redoubtable *glory of the Lord*," manifested time and again, whenever God drew near to man in the Old Testament?

MYSTERY OF THE CHURCH

No early Christian could have been insensitive to the fact that the *"glory of the Lord"* which shone *"round about"* (Lk 2:9) the shepherds on the night of the Lord's Nativity was a confirmation that the God of Abraham, Isaac and Jacob, the God of Moses and Elijah, was once again drawing nigh to man in the birth of Him who was the Incarnation of His Only-Begotten Son and Word: Jesus Christ. That same glory was again manifest at His Baptism, at His Transfiguration, and at His Resurrection. Today, by God's grace, it continues to be manifested within Orthodoxy. In Orthodox history we have seen such a manifestation became a part of St. Seraphim of Sarov's legacy to the world, reassuringly illustrating his teaching that the purpose of life is to *"acquire the Holy Spirit."*

The glory of Jesus Christ manifested in the New Testament is thus not only one and the same glory as the glory of the Lord manifested in the Old Testament, but, by the grace of God, is still consciously cherished and can be experienced within the Orthodox Church. In contrast with the fallen state of the created order, where all ends in the darkness and decay of death, the eternal glory of God burns with dynamic power at the very heart of the mystery of the Church in Orthodoxy.

ii

No feast in Orthodoxy, with the notable exception of Holy Pascha (Easter), seems fuller of the "right glory" than the "Theophany", the feast of the "appearance of God," celebrated each year on January 6. Preceded by a vigil of strict fasting on January 5, it coincides in the West with the celebration of the Epiphany, a coincidence of dates thoroughly confusing to any western Christian attempting to accommodate western thought-patterns to this so purely Orthodox feast.

Pascha (Easter) was celebrated at the time of the Jewish Passover at the very beginning of Christianity, it being the yearly anniversary of Jesus Christ's crucifixion, death, and resurrection. Did St. Paul not write to the Corinthians: *"Christ our Passover is sacrificed for us: therefore let us keep the feast"* (I Cor 5:7-8)? But apart from Pascha/Passover, the oldest celebration known in the pre-Constantinian Church, and one not borrowed from Judaism, was the feast of the baptism of Christ on January 6. It was well in place prior to the fourth century development of other calendar feasts such as Christmas and the Annunciation. Its venerability is moreover echoed to this day in the astounding proportions the celebration of Christ's baptism still takes on in a non-Byzantine church such as that of Ethiopia.

When, however, a Western Christian discovers that the great and solemn Orthodox celebration on January 6 is solely centered on the Baptism of Christ, making no mention whatsoever of the Wise Men, his western culture usually rebels. The concept of the twelve days of Christmas is deeply rooted in the West, thanks to a popular English Christmas carol and Shakespeare's well-known play, "Twelfth Night." In France the "Feast of the Three Kings" on January 6 is universally celebrated with a special cake, sold in bakeries with a gold-paper crown for the "king" or "queen" to be discerned at the feast.

When first challenged by this radical divergence of Orthodoxy concerning the celebration of January 6, Western

MYSTERY OF THE CHURCH

Christians, quietly confident that Orthodoxy really has nothing to do with their own, quite adequate Christianity, may tend to dismiss Orthodoxy's imposing celebration of the Baptism of Christ with an indifferent shrug. In any case, of what possible importance could the Baptism of Christ really have?

The Western Christian, even if sympathetic to Orthodoxy, would therefore feel amply justified in belaboring the Orthodox for "playing down" Christmas. Do they not lump the adoration of the Magi with the adoration of the shepherds both in the liturgical texts for December 25 and in the icons of the Nativity? In any case, the Westerner is pacified in learning that, with or without the Magi's coming being celebrated on January 6, the fast-free period following Christmas is also kept in Orthodoxy up until the strict fast of January 5!

That Western Christians should have such reactions to the reality of the Orthodox celebration of January 6 graphically underlines, of course, how fundamentally different Orthodox emphasis is from that of Western Christianity. For January 6 celebrates Orthodoxy's most essential mystery: the "right glory" of God, Father, Son and Holy Spirit, first revealed at the baptism of Christ in the waters of the Jordan.

iii

At the baptism of Jesus Christ by St. John the Baptist, the Father's voice spoke, bearing witness to Him as His Son, while the Holy Spirit, in the likeness of a dove, alighted on Him. The mystery of God as Holy Trinity was thus explicitly announced and the "*true Light*" of the "*true faith*" of Orthodoxy publicly manifested. Also publicly confirmed in this "theophany" or "appearance of God," was the divinity of Jesus Christ, as second Person of the Holy Trinity, the Son and Word of God, at last appearing on earth in human flesh. Orthodox's perspective on this singular event illuminates why both the first and the last written of the four Gospels, Mark and John, respectively, begin not with the birth of Christ, but with His baptism. With no hesitation whatsoever both immediately address primitive Christianity's most astounding claims: Jesus Christ was God incarnate and the Holy Trinity was fully revealed to mankind for the first time at the moment of His baptism in the Jordan, just prior to His beginning His public ministry.

The manifestation of the identity of Jesus Christ at His baptism was therefore also a revelation concerning the uncreated, triune nature of the one, true God. Henceforth Christianity's monotheism would be easily distinguishable from all others by a great, personal intimacy characterizing the relationship between man and God. The Word made flesh would teach man to address God as "Our Father."

Since the startlingly new revelation of God's triune nature was to emerge from Christ's baptism, it is not insignificant that, within the divine economy, the baptizer of Christ was foreordained to be a notable personage in the old religion, one whom the Jews themselves acknowledged as the last of their great prophets: John the Baptist. This last and greatest of the Jewish prophets however deferred to the much fuller revelation of God brought into the world by Christ:

MYSTERY OF THE CHURCH

"This is he of whom I said, After me cometh a man which is preferred before me: for he was before me. And I knew him not: but that he should be made manifest to Israel, therefore am I come baptizing with water. And John bare record, saying, I saw the Spirit descending from heaven like a dove, and it abode upon him." (Jn 1: 30-32)

In Orthodoxy St. John the Baptist is much venerated and invariably spoken of as "the Forerunner." Was it not said of him by the Lord himself: *"Among them that are born of women there hath not risen a greater than John the Baptist"* (Mat 11:11)? On the iconostasis in Greek churches he, as the *"friend of the Bridegroom"* (Jn 3:29), has his icon situated on the left of the icon of the Bridegroom of the Church, Jesus Christ, just as the icon of the most holy Godbirthgiver is always on His right, fulfilling the Psalmist's prophecy: *"King's daughters were among thy honourable women: upon thy right hand did stand the queen"* (Ps 45:9).

Both Mark's and John's Gospels from their first chapters are indeed postulated on these two evangelists' grasp of the truly cosmic dimension accorded human history by the entrance of Jesus Christ into it as God in the flesh, and by the ensuing revelation of the Holy Trinity. Only St. John, however, tells of St. John the Baptist's proclamation that He whom he baptized was the divine and sacrificial *"Lamb of God"* who was *"to take away the sins of the world"* (Jn 1:20).

The mystery of the *"Lamb of God,"* who was *"to take away the sins of the world,"* is inextricably tied to the mystery of Jesus Christ as God since, to be universally efficacious, the sacrifice of the Lamb of God had to be accomplished by none other than by God Himself. Thus through the offering made by the only-begotten Son and Word of God in Jesus Christ it was given man to behold Him suffering fully in His humanity, yet in a humanity inextricably and eternally joined to His divinity, in which, as One of the Holy Trinity, He did not suffer. It is His suffering humanity and death, however, that allows Him to become identifiable with the whole of the human race. It is through His suffering humanity that He assimilates and assumes forever the suffering of the whole human race stretching from the beginning to the end of time. He thereby became the spotless propitiation for the sins of the world, the passover for all who believe in His Name. For He is indeed the true Lamb of God, *"slain from the foundation of the world"* (Rev :13), as St. John the Theologian would proclaim in his final Revelation of the mysteries of God.

Were his identity other than that of the Son of God, how could He take away the sins of the world, trampling down death by death through His descent into Hades? Many just men have offered their lives for others. Only He, however, the Son of God, the only-begotten of His Father before all worlds, could, in His incarnate, crucified human body, descend to preach to those in Hades, and by the sheer glory of His presence there, completely harrow it.

On this point Orthodoxy distinguishes herself from the heterodox by going far beyond the much simpler concept of the mere redemption of human sin by the crucifixion. In Orthodoxy there is an insistence on the cosmic aspects of this redemptive action which was to destroy the power death had formerly held over mankind. His redemption of the race from death was moreover announced to the dead on the evening of Good Friday. For the glory of what He had accomplished was retroactive, renewing all fallen creation.

As we have previously remarked, one sings in the resurrection hymn for the sixth tone: "*Thou didst slay hell with the splendour of thy godhead.*" Again, as St. John Chrysostom says in his Easter sermon, a fixed liturgical text read during the celebration of Orthodox Pascha: Hades "*took a body, and lo! it discovered God. It took earth, and, behold! it encountered Heaven. It took what it saw, and was overcome by what it did not see.*"

It was therefore to protect the absolute universality of His offering for the whole human race that a saint such as St. Athanasius fought, and at so great a cost to himself, against the errors of Arius who refused to acknowledge that Jesus Christ was "*of one essence with the Father*" and was therefore indeed God who, through the Virgin Mary, joined perfect divinity with perfect humanity. Speaking of that human nature assumed by God in Jesus Christ, St. Gregory of Nazianzus observed: "*What has been assumed has been redeemed, and what has been united to God has been saved.*" Thus was man saved indeed by Jesus Christ through the perfect union in one Person of His suffering humanity and the non-suffering of His divinity as the Second Person of the Holy Trinity.

As we have seen, St. Gregory of Sinai has defined "*true Orthodoxy,*" as true knowledge of these two basic mysteries of the holy Orthodox Faith. The icon of the Theophany, or Baptism of Christ, gives us a true image of that "true Orthodoxy" of which St. Gregory of Sinai spoke. The divine and human natures are both incarnate in the one person of

MYSTERY OF THE CHURCH

Jesus Christ, and the triune nature of the one God is expressed
by the voice of the Father acknowledging the Son on Whom
the Dove descended.

iv

The pious Orthodox soul has no difficulty in
understanding the seventeenth chapter of St. John's Gospel as
a burning, dynamic and eternal intercession for the "right
glory" of Orthodoxy itself.   Therein is found the
extraordinarily mystical text of the Lord's high priestly prayer
for his disciples, a text divinely revealed to the beloved John
who, like Peter and James, also slept through the bloody
sweat of the Lord in the garden, as He prayed to be delivered
from the cup of His Passion on the eve of His sacrifice. If
indeed Orthodoxy be the depository of the fullness of "right
glory," regarding these texts as an intercession for Orthodoxy
would certainly seem justified, for this "high priestly prayer"
underlines, with considerable precision, the role played in the
divine economy by the Lord's manifestation to men of the
"doxa"-- or "glory"--of the Father. As His ultimate prayer in
the night in which He was betrayed, and after instituting the
Last Supper, He, as the incarnate Son and Word with no
equivocation whatsoever, invoked the Father:

> *Father, I will that they also, whom thou hast
> given me, be with me where I am, THAT
> THEY MAY BEHOLD MY GLORY, which
> thou has given me: for thou lovedst me before
> the foundation of the world. (Jn 17:24)*

MYSTERY OF THE CHURCH

This text, as indeed this whole extraordinary chapter, thus declares that the coming into the world of Jesus Christ was indeed for the express purpose of showing forth His eternal "right glory" that men might see it. It is moreover, he prays, through His Passion the next day, that He is truly to be glorified. The implication of all this is as disquieting as it is inescapable: His glory is to be found in His suffering. The divine aspect in play here indeed concerns nothing less than the ineffable suffering of incarnate God, about to be offered up the next day *"for the life of the world"* (Jn 6:51). We therefore can draw no conclusion other than that His suffering and His glory are mysteriously linked. But inextricably fused with the redemptive suffering and death which He, in His prayer, is already engaged in accepting-- *"Not my will, but thine be done"* (Lk 11:42)--is also an aspect of the "right glory" of God Himself, such as it is found only in the very bosom of the Father.

> *"I have glorified thee on the earth: I have finished the work which thou gavest me to do. And now, O Father, glorify thou me with thine own self with the glory which I had with thee before the world was. "* (Jn 17:4-5)

The sufferings, death, descent into hell, and resurrection of the Son, about to take place, are therefore forever and inextricably fused with that glory which the Father had given Him *"before the world was."*

This fusion of the Lord's passion and death with the divine glory shared with the Father *"before the world was,"* is further confirmed and clearly emphasized in the Gospel narration of the Lord's Transfiguration on Mt. Tabor. Caught up in the glory of God, He was flanked on either side by Moses and Elijah, representing, respectively, the Law and the Prophets of the Old Covenant God had made with His chosen people. Through the Law and the Prophets the vision of the glory of God had been maintained throughout Jewish history. Now, on this unique occasion, in the full glory of the Lord's transfiguration, these two heavenly figures appear not as silent witnesses, but rather as vocal participants. They "*spake of his decease which he should accomplish at Jerusalem*" (Lk 9:31).

Thus, even in the midst of the heavenly glory of the Uncreated Light of the Transfiguration, those most illustrious representatives of the Law and the Prophets given by the God of Abraham, Isaac and Jacob to His chosen people, were sent to bear witness to the eternal and cosmic significance of the approaching "decease" of Jesus Christ at Jerusalem. They thereby confirmed before the three chosen Apostles on Mt. Tabor that this approaching decease was indeed the divine will and not an unfortunate accident. That "*decease which he should accomplish at Jerusalem*" must forever therefore be associated with the glory they had seen on Mt. Tabor.

This mystical fusion of Jesus Christ's passion and "decease" with the uncreated light and glory of God is further sustained, confirmed and, as it were, crowned by St. John the Theologian in his divine Revelation. St. John, the inspired vessel for recording the Lord's high priestly prayer wherein Jesus Christ prays to be glorified in His Passion, and the only evangelist to report that St. John the Baptist prophetically heralded Him as the "*Lamb of God which taketh away the sin of the world*," returned to that unique image in his Revelation.

69

MYSTERY OF THE CHURCH

There, in his personal mystic vision of last things, he sees Jesus Christ as the immolated Lamb of God, *"slain from the foundation of the world"* (Rev 13:). In this cosmic vision Jesus Christ, the only-begotten of the Father, as the immolated Lamb, is alone found worthy of opening the book to the acclamation of the divine hymn of praise raised by the heavenly choir:

> *"Thou art worthy to take the book, and to open the seals thereof: for thou wast slain and has redeemed us to God by thy blood out of every kindred, and tongue, and people, and nation; and hast made us unto our God kings and priests." (Rev 5:9-10)*

Whenever the mystery of the slain Lamb of God is made incarnate, the fullness of the great mystery of the Church is mystically expressed. The on-going manifestation of the "right glory" in Orthodox martyrs is indeed a continued reenactment of the Lamb's being slain in those belonging to Him. Herein lies the surest manifestation, not only to the Orthodox themselves, but also to the rest of the world, that the Orthodox Church has indeed preserved, intact, the fullness of the "right glory" of the Church of God.

In Orthodoxy, as in St. Paul's writings, it has always been natural for the glorification of the sufferings of the Son to take on fuller incarnate dimensions than those found elsewhere. The many "new martyrs" of recent centuries, so frequently encountered in the daily listings of the Greek *Synaxarion*, repeatedly revealed themselves as individuals who felt called upon to offer their persons to the Turkish authorities as

MYSTERY OF THE CHURCH

Christian victims, freely embracing torture and certain death. They amply illustrate this very deep and mystical side of an Orthodoxy which, far from being rooted in fantasies of the intellect, or in any sort of intellectual conceits--so seductive to educated Western Christians, alas!--draws its strength from the humble, cold reality of the flesh and blood of martyrs. The cult of martyrs was indeed kept very much alive during the long Turkish occupation just as it has been gloriously renewed in this century in the God-hating Socialist regimes in eastern Europe. The fusion of "right glory" with suffering is therefore not only rooted in all the past experience of the Church of God, beginning with the Incarnation of the Son Himself, but has been continuously renewed, and is still being renewed, in the on-going, living experience of those who are Orthodox. Nor can anything in the experience of those first ten centuries, an experience fully shared with the Church of Rome, be said to contradict Orthodox's on-going experience in regard either to martyrdom, or to the willingness of the faithful to embrace it as the crowning of the Christian life. The Crucified Himself is the only prize sought.

An outpost of the Kingdom of the Holy Trinity on earth as well as the true Bride of Christ, the Orthodox Church welcomes those who seek salvation in that kingdom of "right glory" of the Father, Son and Holy Spirit. The glory shining forth from her Bridegroom, Jesus Christ, the veritable incarnation of the Second Person of the Holy Trinity, illuminates the Gospels, the entire New Testament, and indeed the whole world. That same glory still today illuminates the mystery of the Church of God as His bride, as it has ever done. It is indeed the "right glory" of the divine life of the Triune God. By God's mercy "right glory"

71

continues to illumine the Orthodox Church as it is patiently, doggedly lived out by her adherents under her maternal tutelage through the Holy Spirit at work within her. The glory of the Holy Trinity, that is the *"glory of the Lord"* as manifest in Jesus Christ, is thereby fused with the daily life of the Orthodox faithful. It sometimes becomes visible even to the human eye in her saints, martyrs and confessors.

The glory of the Lord in the Old Testament being one and the same glory as the glory of Christ, we are permitted to say that the light and the glory of both the Old and New Testaments do live on in the world today. To behold them one has only to pursue the faithful, suffering witness of the saints of the Orthodox Church. For the glory flowing from them does enlighten all who approach them with fear of God, with faith and love, and with an humble heart, cleansed from passions.

CHAPTER VI

RESURRECTION AND "RIGHT GLORY" IN MARTYRS AND MIRACLES

Never having lost sight of why Christians have always met on Sundays, the Orthodox Church places great emphasis on the primacy of the weekly Divine Liturgy commemorating the Resurrection of Jesus Christ. The myrrh-bearing women who rose up *"very early in the morning the first day of the week"* (Mk 16:2) to go anoint the Lord's body moreover hold a unique place in Orthodox devotion since it was to them, and not to the male disciples, that the Resurrection was first revealed.

Sunday's Divine Liturgy crowns a very distinct liturgical action carried out each weekend in honor of the Resurrection. Since Orthodoxy follows Judaism in beginning the day at sunset of the previous day, the new week's glorification of the Resurrection of Christ begins at Saturday Vespers, continues with Sunday Matins (Orthros), and reaches its climax in the Sunday Divine Liturgy. There the presence of the Resurrected Lord is experienced once again, as by Luke and Cleopas at Emmaus, in *"breaking of bread"* (Lk 24:35).

To provide variety in this weekly glorification of the Resurrection, the Orthodox Church inaugurated eight sets of texts, called the "eight tones," since each one is musically identified with one of Byzantium's eight musical scales. All of these Sunday texts glorify the Passion and Resurrection of Christ, as well as His triumphant slaying of Death through His descent into "hell"--or Hades.

73

MYSTERY OF THE CHURCH

Orthodoxy's weekly emphasis on Christ's descent into hades sometimes startles non-Orthodox observers. This descent, however, was not invented by the Orthodox Church, but was attested to from the beginning by St. Peter himself.

In his first epistle St. Peter speaks of the Lord, after he had been *"put to death in the flesh, but quickened by the Spirit,"* going to preach *"unto the spirits in prison"* (I Pet 3:18-19). This most cosmic aspect of the whole Passion and Resurrection of Christ has however been neglected, if not actually forgotten, in the Christian West where His descent *"unto the spirits in prison"* became overshadowed by juridical preoccupations about how the sacrifice on Calvary accomplished personal salvation from hell.

One of the great and recurring themes for glorification in the Sunday texts of the eight tones is that of God's "Great Mercy" to mankind, even as they also glorify the sufferings and triumph of Christ over Hades and His bringing Adam and Eve and all their descendants out of Death into Life. Whatever the variations found in the music and texts with the eight tones, and however much the original Greek music may be totally replaced by Slavic harmonies or other settings, the thrust of the texts themselves remains unchanged.

Emphasis on the Resurrection is further intensified on Sundays by a special eleven-part cycle based on the eleven Gospel accounts of the Lord's post-Resurrection appearances. One of these eleven accounts is read each week at the very heart of Sunday Matins, followed by the faithful coming forward to kiss the Gospel book. They thereby embrace, as literal truth, the accounts of the Resurrection recorded therein. Comments on that Sunday's Resurrection Gospel are sung at the end of Matins, echoing its literal truth.

MYSTERY OF THE CHURCH

After Sunday Matins have been sung, glorification of the Resurrection stretches towards its mighty climax as the risen Christ, invisibly escorted by angels, stoops to earth once again to be experienced, as we have just seen, in *"breaking of bread"* (Lk 24:35). Through the power of the Holy Spirit the Holy Gifts of bread and wine set forth by the priest and people on the altar become the Body and Blood of Jesus Christ to be communicated to the faithful.

This unchanging weekly emphasis on experiencing, every Sunday, the presence of the living Christ who conquered Hades and rose from the dead, reminds believers that the "Great Time" of Jesus Christ has never past, and that, just as He promised, He is with those who are His to the end of time. Confidently Orthodox believers exchange a very Orthodox greeting as they embrace one another:

"Christ is in our midst!"

"He is, and will ever be!"

Regular participation in Sunday worship closely binds all Orthodox Christians into one dynamic mystical body through the Holy Spirit. Thereby is sustained, within the mystery of the Church, the deep communion Orthodoxy has always felt with her saints and martyrs, past and present. It is this deep communion which nurtures the vocation to be a witness--a "martyr" in Greek --for the "right glory" of Orthodoxy.

ii

The martyr's witness of St. Ignatius, second Bishop of Antioch, at the beginning of the second century still burns brightly in Orthodoxy memory. St. Peter himself had founded the church in that great metropolis where *"the disciples were called Christians first"* (Acts 11:26). St. Ignatius's witness in the early Apostolic Church, and the touching reaction by the Christians of his time to that witness, proves helpful moreover in understanding what the "right glory" of Orthodoxy is all about.

Ignatius had been a disciple of John, the beloved disciple, and was highly esteemed by the faithful of Antioch as their Bishop. He encouraged those who witnessed as martyrs, greatly admiring them. He himself had never been arrested, however, in spite of the sporadic persecutions by the Roman government, intermittently launched against the Christian "atheists" for refusing to offer incense to the gods of Rome. Around the year 113, however, less than a century after the Resurrection of the Lord, the Emperor Trajan stopped off in Antioch with his troops, and unleashed a violent campaign against the city's prominent Christians. Ignatius, sensing he would be taken, appeared before the Emperor of the mighty Roman Empire without waiting to be arrested.

Keenly aware that the bishop of the trouble-making Christians now stood before him, unafraid and of his own free will, Trajan asked:

"So you are a disciple of Him who was crucified under Pontius Pilate?"

Ignatius calmly replied: *"I am the disciple of Him who nailed my sin to the Cross, and who trampled down the devil and his machinations."*

Having heard of the bishop's reputation among the Christians, Trajan asked curiously: *"Why do they call you the 'God-bearer'"?*

MYSTERY OF THE CHURCH

"Because, within me, I bear the living Christ," Ignatius replied.

As if to crush "the living Christ" Himself, the Emperor issued his brutal order to the guards:

"Let him who bears the Crucified One be taken to Rome in chains and fed to the lions for the people's entertainment." Ignatius actually kissed the heavy chains with which the guards bound him, calling them his *"most precious spiritual pearls,"* for they allowed him to follow the example of St. Paul. They were a sign, a precious ornament announcing to all that he was soon to gain that prize for which he longed above all earthly comforts: Christ Himself.

Dispatched on foot, Antioch's God-bearing bishop was escorted by an unsympathetic Roman guard. We know from epistles he dispatched along the way that he deeply pondered the final bloody scene in the Roman arena where, in one last liturgy of glory, he would simultaneously be both the priest who was sacrificing, and the victim being sacrificed. He moreover expressed, in a letter sent ahead to the faithful in Rome, his burning desire to accomplish this final witness without hindrance. Strongly opposing any thoughts the Roman Christians might have about intervening, he pled with them: *"Allow me to become an imitator of the passion of my God. [...] Let me become the food of the beasts through whom it will be possible for me to find God. I am God's wheat and the teeth of the beasts will grind me so that I may be found a pure loaf for Christ."*

Asia Minor, through which the Roman guard escorted Ignatius, boasted many Christians, having been evangelized from the beginning by Paul and other of the Apostles. As word spread that the God-bearing Bishop of Antioch,

77

Ignatius, was on his way to Rome to witness in the arena, the faithful poured out to venerate the future martyr.

At Smyrna there was a particularly poignant meeting with Smyrna's bishop, Polycarp, his much younger fellow-disciple of John the beloved. Polycarp had accompanied their master into banishment on Patmos two decades before. Now, very briefly, he could draw grace and strength from the witness of the older Ignatius. Many years hence and at past eighty years of age, Polycarp too would bear his own witness in the Roman arena at Smyrna where he would die on the pyre.

During the halt in Smyrna other neighboring bishops also came there to greet Ignatius and seek his blessing. Antioch's God-bearer left Smyrna for Rome, it is said, not as one condemned to death, but as an athlete on his way to win a coveted prize.

Yet the "right glory" emanating from Ignatius seemed even more abundant once his martyrdom was complete. Christians in Rome piously heeded his admonitions not to interfere, allowing him to become "*food for those beasts*" and "*a pure loaf for Christ.*" After assisting at his final liturgy to the glory of God, however, they did slip surreptitiously into the arena and gathered up the few large bones left by the beasts, wrapping them in fine cloth as martyr's relics and piously dispatched them back to the faithful of Antioch.

St. Ignatius's relics thus retraced the route he himself had made so shortly before, bound by his "*most precious spiritual pearls.*" At their passage they were greeted with an even greater triumph than that greeting the martyr in chains. Were these relics not tangible proof of the victory of the resurrected Christ who had conquered natural frailty in Ignatius' flesh and blood? By the power of God he had won the prize he coveted.

Venerating his relics with love and awe, the faithful accepted miracles and wonders emanating from them as something natural and not at all surprising or extraordinary. In the primitive church, as in the Orthodox Church today, miracles and wonders emanating from relics were understood as quiet confirmations of the "right glory" of God at work within the mystery of the Church through the power of the Holy Spirit.

iii

The "right glory" of miracles proves far less problematic for the Orthodox than for most heterodox believers, be they Catholic or Protestant. It was undeniably a part of the apostolic experience described by St. Luke in the Book of Acts and still an ever-relevant experience within the Church of God.

An Orthodox Christian never speaks of New Testament times as being "the time of miracles" nor of a contemporary miracle as being a "modern" miracle. Such commonly heard expressions betray the profound dichotomy that has crept into Western Christian thinking regarding "then" and "now." In Orthodoxy there is only one time, the time of God, which is always an eternal "now."

Whatever else may be said of miracles, it is obvious that they cannot belong to the temporal order: they partake of the eternity of God Himself. The French philosopher Simone Weil wryly observed that miracles do not violate "natural law," they merely prove that we do not know what "natural law" is.

Whatever the restrictions imposed by time and space in this world, the lover of God understands that ultimate reality is rooted in something beyond this world and its restrictions. For such a believer no law can impede the expression of the eternal and infinite dimensions of the divine energies of God at work in His creation, for "*With God all things are possible*" (Mat 19:26).

Orthodoxy has never felt any need either to question the apostolic tradition of miracles or, in an embarrassed attempt to be "modern," turn her back on that tradition. Shame of one's origins is not applicable to the Orthodox Church which knows her ultimate dependency is ever on God alone. By God's grace Orthodoxy was spared the Renaissance by which both Apostolic Christianity and the lordship of Christ were betrayed through humanism's lordship of man and the promise of building a better world than the one given by God.

Miracles are therefore just a normal part of the timeless life in God to which the Orthodox Church bears witness in her role as an earthly outpost of the Kingdom of the Holy Trinity. They are humbly accepted as graces of God and considered a mere part of a far more general manifestation of God's glory to be experienced through His divine energies at work within the mystery of the Church. Miracles have no need either to be proven or disproved. If something wondrous occurs, one humbly gives glory to God, regardless of how great or how small. If something wondrous does not occur, one still humbly gives glory to God, for all is given by God and can only happen within His divine economy. As the dying twenty-four year-old Thérèse of Lisieux (1873-1897) replied, when one of her curious Carmelite sisters insensitively asked her what she would do, should she die suddenly without having received the sacraments: *"Receiving the Sacraments is a great grace if it is willed by God. But if God does not will it, that too is grace. Everything is grace."*

The Lord did indeed come into the world to *show forth* that glory He shared with the Father before the world came into being (Jn 17:5). Throughout the centuries those who love Him, and are His, continue to bear witness to that very basic dogmatic truth. Orthodox Matins begins with the repeatedly sung declaration: *"God is the Lord and hath appeared unto us! Blessed is He that cometh in the Name of the Lord!"*

It is for this reason that insisting that "Orthodox" means "right glory" rather than "right teaching" or "right thinking" is not a negligible detail. It is of fundamental importance for any non-Orthodox approaching Orthodoxy and sincerely seeking to grasp the mystery of the Church. "Right teaching" or "right thinking" require only intellectual assent, that is, the exercise of one's mind and will alone, giving one a purely human approach to God. For the intellectual, of course, this disincarnate approach seems a normal one, indeed the only one which he, an intellectual, could possible conceive.

Intellectual assent to "right teaching" or "right doctrine," however, with no deep involvement of the heart, allows one the very questionable freedom of functioning on an intellectual level alone. Daily participation in the "right glory" of the divine life for those who have *"put on Christ"* (Gal 3:27) in baptism requires something far more thoroughgoing than the mere exercise of a disincarnate human mind.

MYSTERY OF THE CHURCH

"Right glory" includes both body and soul and involves the whole person. However well-educated it may be, the human intellect, no less than the human body, must, through a long austerity of ascetical striving out of love for Jesus Christ, learn to submit the whirlwind of its hyper-active mental preoccupations to serving God in all things, and above all things. The glory and holiness of God is the only goal.

Whether seen in a famous saint, or in just any man, "right glory" is always the manifestation of God at work in him, demonstrating that, through love of God, human flesh and blood can be sanctified by the Holy Spirit working within man's heart. Yet glory, like the holiness of God, of which it is a manifestation, even though visible and perceivable by man, and even though partaken of and manifested by man--as in the case of St. Seraphim of Sarov--, nonetheless still retains something of the illusive nature of the invisibility of the Holy Spirit. It can never be captured, labeled, measured or classified as if it were a specimen for analysis. Did the Lord not compare the Holy Spirit to the wind when he said to Nicodemus: *"The wind bloweth where it listeth, and thou hearest the sound thereof, but canst not tell whence it cometh"* (Jn 3:8)?

Since one partakes of glory, as of holiness, only within the Holy Spirit and through love, such love must be a genuine love of the heart, a love so strong that the whole body feels constrained to reflect it. Whence Orthodoxy's constant reminders about fasting which, if done out of love, is indeed an offering of the heart.

Has God not willed that man seek Him above all else through his heart? *"A broken and contrite heart, O God, thou wilt not despise"* (Ps 51:17), the Psalmist states. From

82

apostolic times belief with all one's heart has been deemed necessary for Christian salvation. Did Philip not reply to the Ethiopian eunuch, when asked if he might be baptized: "*If thou believest with all thine heart, thou mayest*" (Acts 8:37)?

That is why glory defies all attempts to capture it and make it one's own, except by the straight path of loving asceticism. Unless one lovingly seek glory with humility, faith, hope and fear of God, both holiness and its glory will remain illusive, regardless of how much one may go through the motions of Orthodox worship, keeping all the feasts and fasts and attending all the services of Lent. The heart must be involved. For, within the mystery of the Church, when the heart is open to God, the splendor of the holy glory of Jesus Christ is conveyed and is made incarnate by those who have "*put on Christ*" (Gal 3:27) in baptism, and in whose hearts His name has been sealed by the Spirit. They have been called to live in the Kingdom of the Resurrected Christ not just outwardly, but inwardly.

Today, as it has ever been, the living proof of the presence of the Holy Spirit in Orthodoxy is its continued visibility through the witness of her saints, martyrs and confessors. The sheer number of Orthodox martyrs offered up to God in the twentieth century as the "*first-fruits of the universe,*" undoubtedly surpasses that of any previous century. As has been true from the beginning of Christianity, these twentieth-century Orthodox martyrs for Jesus Christ also have provided a true cross-cut of society. In twentieth-century Russia one finds not only humble peasants and workers slaughtered for their faith, but also members of the highest aristocracy of Europe. The Grand Duchess Elizabeth, grand-daughter of Queen Victoria and sister of the last Tzarina, a German

Protestant convert, was much given to works of mercy and, following her husband's assassination, was consecrated a nun. Her royal martyr's blood was mingled with that of believers of far humbler birth.

It is a curious footnote to the Christian history of the twentieth century that at its end, entombed in Jerusalem in the Russian convent on the Mount of Olives, beside the miraculously preserved and myrrh-gushing relics of the Grand Duchess Elizabeth, there lies the body of the mother-in-law of the Queen of England, Prince Philip's Greek mother. Niece of the Grand Duchess Elizabeth, whom she deeply venerated and whose witness she wished to emulate, she became a nun in Greece where she also founded a monastery and practiced works of mercy. Her final request was that her body finally repose in Jerusalem next to the holy relics of her martyred aunt.

Regardless of birth or fortune or education, the most intimate bond possible between all Orthodox Christians is their mutual union with Jesus Christ whereby the "right glory" of the Holy Trinity continues to be seen. Though this world be ruled by the Prince of Darkness, the blood of the martyrs holds his dark forces at bay by the power of the resurrected Christ living in them.

iv

One understands that the mystery of the Church, as experienced by the believer, cannot but be fused with the "right glory" of the Holy Trinity which ever encompasses the risen Christ. Such glory in fact unfailingly bears witness to a certain intimacy with Him who has risen from the dead. It is moreover this growing intimacy with the resurrected Christ that sustains the Orthodox believer who humbly accepts that Jesus Christ is indeed *"the Way, the Truth, and the Life"* (Jn 14:6). By Him, through Him, and with Him alone is one led into the Kingdom of the Holy Trinity.

As the priest elevates the just-consecrated Gifts at the Divine Liturgy, he exclaims in a loud voice: *"Holy things are for the holy!"* The very Orthodox reply sung back is: *"One is holy! One is Lord! Jesus Christ! To the glory of God the Father! Amen!"* It is only to the extent that one is in Jesus Christ that one becomes holy and filled with the "right glory." Apart from Jesus Christ, neither holiness nor "right glory" is conceivable, for saints are not made by canonizations, but by the living Christ they bear within themselves. Like St. Ignatius of Antioch, saints are "God-bearers." If an Orthodox Christian be faithful to the vows of his baptism that is the goal towards which he strives.

It is not therefore just within oneself, nor just for oneself that an Orthodox Christian strives to be a living member of the Mystical Body of Christ which is the Church. He is ever mindful that he is but a lowly participant joined with countless other members of that Body as he prays each week at the Divine Liturgy.

In the case of hermits, or of penitents such as St. Mary of Egypt, who find themselves physically cut off from the Divine Liturgy on Sundays, they prove themselves all the more aware of the necessity of uniting their prayer and personal ascetical efforts to those divine energies released throughout the world by the millions of Divine Liturgies being offered up to God in the world, and for the world. No hermit or penitent, no matter how cut off from society around them, would ever think of praying apart from the mystery of the Church which ever burns steadily within their hearts. After 47 years of isolated penance known to God alone, one of the first inquiries of St. Mary of Egypt to Fr. Zossima was to ask how the Church of God was faring in the world. She whose prayer was so ardent that Fr. Zossima saw her lifted above the ground when she stretched out her hands to God to intercede for the world, had therefore not at all lived apart from the mystery of the Church in her desert for 47 years. Rather was her prayer and suffering at the very heart of it, sustaining it and raising it up before the Father's face as she herself became an incarnation of that mystery.

The faithful Orthodox soul patiently practices his faith while awaiting a total transfiguration by the divine energies, in order that the "right glory" of the Uncreated Light manifested both on Mount Tabor and at the Resurrection, might shine forth, however humbly, from him. For that end he strives, fasts and prays. It is for that end alone, after all, that he was born, that he exists, and has his being, whatever may be the defeats or vicissitudes of his life on earth. Whether one dies in peace in one's bed, or violently as a martyr, the faithful soul's vocation is unchanging within the mystery of the Church: to witness, through the indwelling of the Holy Spirit, that Jesus Christ is the Son of the living God, that the glory of the Father might be made manifest before men.

CHAPTER VII

PERSONAL VOCATION WITHIN THE MYSTERY

Jesus Christ personally called individuals to come follow him. Each in his own way answered that personal summons according to his heart's disposition. Nor was that personal call limited to those to whom He actually spoke. Some, merely by looking upon Him, heard a call in their hearts to give themselves to Him. Others, even at a distance, found their hearts respond from merely having heard speak of Him, mysteriously sensing that in Him was the answer to all their longings and difficulties. Did He not say that those who believe in Him without having seen Him are blessed (Jn 20:29)?

However a believer is called, the answer must be associated with his heart's affections. The rich young man, whom the Lord looked upon and loved, turned and walked away when told that to be perfect he must sell all his goods and come and follow Him (Mat 19:16-22). Judas Iscariot was called as one of His twelve intimates but his heart too was tied to love of money and he sold the Lord of Glory for thirty pieces of silver. Personal rapport between the believer's own heart and the Lord who calls proves an indispensable element in discipleship.

The teaching of St. Paul emphasizes personal intimacy with Jesus Christ to the extent that he wrote: *"I live; yet not I, but Christ liveth in me"* (Gal. 2:20). He insisted also that *"as many of you as have been baptized into Christ have put on Christ"* (Gal 3:27), each one, for himself. It is indeed individual Christians who make up the Body of Christ which

87

is the Church and, within the mystery of the Church, are each "*members in particular*" (I Cor 12:27) of that Body.

Since what is of God is eternal and unchanging, the heart's answer to the call of Christ is still the same today as during the reign of Tiberius Caesar when the Lord, walking the face of Palestine, spoke to human hearts, with or without words. Thus, whatever it may be with the mass conversions on the day of Pentecost, the appeal to each soul was, even then, still essentially personal, for "*every man heard them speak in his own language*" (Acts 2:6). Hearing the fullness of Christ proclaimed in one's own language still proves the ultimate in "personalized" appeal, as many Orthodox converts can attest upon recalling the first Divine Liturgy they heard celebrated in a language they could understand. Every Orthodox believer is called to an intimate relationship with Jesus Christ. This lies at the very heart of the mystery of the Church. If the glory of the Father is to shine forth from such intimacy, it must be cherished, nurtured and cultivated however, just as intimacy in marriage. Indeed, the glory of intimacy with Jesus Christ in the on-going life of Orthodox Christians is, within the mystery of the Church, a characteristic always to be found in Holy Tradition.

ii

Given this orientation towards intimacy with Christ, it is hardly surprising that the monastic ideal plays such a powerful role amongst the pious Orthodox laity. This is hard for non-Orthodox to grasp, even for Roman Catholics who usually imagine monasticism solidly fused--not to say confused--with the concept of "religious orders," a concept utterly foreign to Orthodoxy. The concept of monasticism *per se,* as guarded in Orthodoxy, has been all but lost in the popular mind in the West. It is of course cherished in certain western monasteries conscious of the East's great tradition and is patently evident in the *Rule* of St. Benedict. For the Orthodox faithful monasticism remains an ideal, inspiring and nourishing their ecclesial life. Monks and nuns are generally regarded as the conscious guardians of the holy Orthodox faith as they attempt to make it incarnate in their lives. It was from this high regard for monasticism that arose the now venerable tradition of drawing Orthodoxy's bishops exclusively from the monastic ranks.

Indeed, "the angelic life" of the monastic is viewed as a normal, and not an exceptional, goal for anyone really intent upon pursuing the divine life of a Christian in all its fullness, though it will never be, and never has been embraced by other than a minority of believers. Nonetheless, the monastic vocation is honored as the crowning of the Christian life and esteemed as a "higher" vocation than marriage. Yet marriage and monasticism are both solemnly crowned by the Orthodox Church as consecrated states in which one will answer for one's life before the throne of God: the married person as the spouse of another; the monastic as the spouse of God.

Though for various reasons pious souls may find themselves unable to embrace the monastic life, they will often increasingly seek after the "angelic life" of the monk or nun in their married or single state. They may intensify, as their commitments allow them, their attempt to "pray without ceasing" through the Jesus Prayer. They may adopt a more austere style of life, or even withdraw more and more from worldly activities for increased prayer and good works.

MYSTERY OF THE CHURCH

Hungry for the experience of God, pious Orthodox souls also tend to seek out those who, through their experience, have gained a certain intimacy with God. Often they may come to regard them as spiritual fathers or mothers to whom they owe obedience. Recent years have seen countless souls in the United States and Canada turning to an Athonite elder who, after a very charismatic witness as one of the twenty ruling Abbots on Mount Athos, and a monastic reformer both on Athos and in Greece itself, has gone about founding both men's and women's monasteries in North America.

Even in our own times we are thus seeing the outpouring of the Holy Spirit in North America as monasticism takes root according to the most venerated monastic tradition. Athonite monasticism is no longer limited to the Holy Mountain of Athos. In this particular case the elder's spiritual direction has been extended far beyond those hundreds of spiritual children he already counted on the Holy Mountain and in Greece before coming to North America.

Certainly one cannot pretend that organized monasticism existed from the beginning of the Church, even if one discerns the presence of the "angelic life" in such prophets as Elijah and John the Baptist who lived in solitude before God. Monastic communities were however a natural response to the relative ease of living as a Christian once the sporadic, but implacable rash of violent persecutions throughout the Church's first three centuries had come to an end. "Martyr" means "witness" in Greek, and monasticism became a new sort of "witness." The witness of the monk ever looking towards heaven today still challenges man's forgetfulness that the temporal glories of this world are passing.

MYSTERY OF THE CHURCH

iii

Within the mystery of the Church, Orthodox believers, both married and monastic, are solemnly crowned before God as both *"kings and priests"* (Rev 5:10). They are thus, each of them, fully responsible for manifesting the "right glory" of the resurrected Christ to the world in that crowned state. Still the mystery of the Church is never conditioned by, nor confined to, the behavior of any one of its members, whatever his ecclesiastical rank. When Peter, chief of the Apostles, abandoned the cross, the fullness of the "right glory" within the mystery of the Church was still manifested by the confession of the dying thief, as also by the confession of the centurion who pierced His side. In the mystery of the Church the confession of the humblest Orthodox convert is as rooted in the fullness of holy Orthodoxy as is the confession of the Ecumenical Patriarch.

Yet personal responsibility for the fullness of Christ as an Orthodox Christian never leads to Protestantism. Even though an Orthodox Christian is allowed complete freedom to struggle with the problem of being a rational creature who may find himself tempted to question God, he will never attempt to live by his own reasoning alone. As an Orthodox Christian he must stay open to the whole of the Church's past, ever striving to embrace it and make it a part of his own personal history. He honors this whole, knowing it to be an ever-pertinent frame of reference for his own present. Indeed, the present conflict at any particular time is seldom one for which some ancient parallel cannot be found. This, of course, is in complete contrast with the humanist Western Christian orientation. Fashioned by the Reformation or the Counter-

MYSTERY OF THE CHURCH

Reformation, and imbued with ideas of "progress" and "the modern," Western Christians are often embarrassed by the "superstitions" of their Christian past when uneducated monks worked miracles and were venerated by the masses. Shame of one's origins tends to dominate the Catholic view of the Church today with frequent apologies for "unenlightened" or "inappropriate" actions, and for beliefs manifested by a more "primitive" Christianity, while one clamors for even more "enlightened" measures to be taken. Holy Orthodoxy, on the other hand, has no choice: she is that scorned and "unenlightened" primitive Christianity.

How many times has the "post-Vatican II Church" not been held up for adulation over the past thirty years as "new and improved" Catholicism, while one blushingly tries to change history by veiling over what the pre-Vatican II Church was? Living with such a dichotomy in one's own religious psyche regarding the wholeness of the mystery of the Church is, in addition to being basically dishonest, also very far from that fullness of Christ in His Church as attested to by Orthodoxy.

Orthodoxy's faithful seem instinctively aware that history is not broken in its continuity. Neither the violent humanist distortions of the Renaissance and Reformation, nor their nefarious myths of "progress" and "the modern" have penetrated the mystic depths of the Orthodox psyche. This is why many Orthodox say that Catholicism and Protestantism have more in common with one another than either does with Orthodoxy.

"Progress" and "the modern" are so firmly entrenched in western civilization as virtues that people embracing western civilization automatically embrace both myths. They aspire to become "westernized" and join in a civilization which, considering the production of nuclear waste alone, pursues, selfishly and callously, in the name of economic progress, the demonic design of perverting and spoiling, for thousands of years to come, greater and greater portions of God's creation, leaving those who inherit these perverted, spoiled portions an abomination of desolation.

iv

Not by her merits but by the grace of God did the Orthodox Church escape the revamping and the "bringing up to date" that the Latin Church imposed upon itself with the Councils of Trent, Vatican I, and Vatican II. Orthodoxy in contrast makes it possible for her faithful to savor the depths of the countless possibilities found in Holy Tradition for leading one's personal life in Christ. For Orthodoxy's history is vast, her saints are many.

Obviously no one saint can contain the whole of the mystery of the Church. One will moreover naturally be more drawn to the mystery as revealed in certain of God's holy ones than in others. Yet in regard to the saints with whom one becomes intimate, one is never championed against another: all are servants of Christ Who Himself is the only goal, the only crown sought by each of them. Humbly and prayerfully the Orthodox soul reads the Lord's words: *"In my Father's house are many mansions"* (Jn 14:2).

The on-going witness of God's holy ones continues to prove each of them unique. By their common transfiguration in Christ, through the Holy Spirit, every saint is however joined with the others in forming a *"great a cloud of witnesses"* (Heb 12:1), hovering over the Church, protecting it and interceding for it. All bear witness to the "right glory" of the human race and is an unique incarnation of the "right glory" given him. Each saint therefore, seen or unseen, known or unknown to all save God, constitutes a priceless, eternal thread by which the tapestry of the divine economy is woven. In God nothing holy is ever lost. Within the mystery of the Church, one's life in Christ, *"hid with Christ in God"* (Col 3:3), is indeed part of that eternal tapestry, a tapestry not woven by human hands, but by the Holy Spirit, through Jesus Christ, to the glory of the Father.

Increasing familiarity with the great Orthodox souls of the past initiates the believer into living within Holy Tradition. Through the mystery of the Church he learns to join in their eternal intercession, for they are ever-present in holy Orthodoxy, permeating the perverted order of this fallen planet by converting those sinful believers in whose hearts their memory takes root and dwells. Holding fast to the whole of the Christian past contained within Holy Tradition, the Orthodox Church protects both herself and her faithful from demonic illusions of "progress" and "the modern." At the same time she continues to make available to Christians of today all the vast richness and variety of "right glory" witness to the fullness of Christ which, by God's grace, is deposited in her.

v

The divine warfare between the Prince of this world and the Kingdom of the Holy Trinity, of course, is unavoidable for the Orthodox believer as he finds himself drawn ever

94

more deeply into the mystery of the Church. He increasingly becomes aware of the demonic powers conniving for his own soul, as also for the soul of every believer. He discovers himself engaged, willingly or unwillingly, in an on-going battle lasting until his last breath. Indeed, from the moment of his baptism, a believer is engaged in a struggle where he himself is the disputed prey, often without his even being aware of it. But whenever he starts to *"put away childish things"* (I Cor 13:11), he becomes increasingly open to the great wisdom of the holy Fathers and Mothers in their admonitions to fast and pray. He begins to grasp that such admonitions are pertinent to all believers, and not just to monastics.

Unflinchingly Orthodoxy has never obscured that such admonitions are valid for all. Through her calendar, so rich with fasts, feasts, commemorations and celebrations, the Orthodox Church does try, in a very general way, to initiate her faithful into the true state of affairs regarding the on-going spiritual battle in which every baptized Christian is engaged. Yet her statutory fasts do not, in themselves, constitute the true fasting of heart and soul whereby the saint intercedes for the world as he struggles to save his own soul. Did St. Seraphim not teach: *"Save yourself and you'll save a thousand?"*

There is a perennial danger for believers to think that "living the life" of an Orthodox Christian can be perfectly accomplished simply by keeping the statutory fasts and feasts of the Orthodox calendar alone. This however is living by the letter of the law and neglecting the apostolic teaching: *"The letter killeth, but the spirit giveth life"* (2 Cor 3:6).

MYSTERY OF THE CHURCH

What is always both essential and vital to this issue is the motivation within the believer's heart for following the calendar's indications. With what comfort do many "strict Orthodox" tend to turn aside from their less strict brethren and pray with the Pharisee: *"God, I thank thee, that I am not as other men are"* (Lk 18:11). Such souls, as the Lord Himself said, *"have their reward"* (Mat 6:2), for they are indeed seen by men, and generally respected, being openly spoken of as "strict Orthodox." But their virtuous feelings and open sense of spiritual merit do not justify them before God as much as the humble, hidden prayer of the sinful publican: *"God be merciful to me a sinner"* (Lk 18:13).

The only valid reason for any ascetical practice is that of personal love for Jesus Christ. This love must be so great that the heart feels compelled to offer Him constantly repeated acts as a means of saying: "I want to do this for you." Repeated daily over the years, these tiny, repeated acts take on a life of their own in the hearts of those who love God. For holiness, within the mystery of the Church, is the fruit of the Holy Spirit who begets Christ in all men, so that they, through their love for Him, may become, as did the Most Holy Theotokos, a vessel for His Incarnation. Through them, in a very small way, and according to the place given them within the divine economy by the grace of the Holy Spirit, His Incarnation is continually being renewed in the world.

The Orthodox Christian looks in a very special way at the "right glory" of the confession of St. Peter, regarding it as a definition of the great mystery of the Church of God on earth. Since it is a Church which can be manifested even where *"two or three are gathered together in [His] name"* (Mat 18:20), we know that Christ's presence in His Church is indeed a mystical and spiritual one, since where He is, there too is the Church. Thus while the Church of God may be seen in all its fullness in the Orthodox Church, the "right glory" can never be limited to Orthodoxy alone.

Nor can "right glory" be limited to any one time period, or to any one culture. The Orthodox Church must remain open to that time in which God has placed her. It is into the present, and not into the past, that the right glory must be incorporated.

The work of the demonic can always be recognized whenever there is any hesitation on the part of the Orthodox in doing this, whatever the challenge, be it language, customs, or even ethnic survival. Reticence on the part of any branch of the Orthodox Church to proclaim to all men, and not just to an ethnic enclave, that Jesus Christ is the Son of the living God, can only be inspired by the Evil One.

We recall therefore once again that the mystical confession of St. Peter: *"Thou art Christ, the Son of the living God"* (Mat 16:16) is the foundation upon which the Church of God was built and, the Lord said, something divinely revealed to St. Peter by the Father Himself (Mat 16:17), and not at all given by the holy Apostle's own lights.

When any Christian confesses with all his heart and soul that Jesus Christ is the *"Son of the Living God,"* both he who confesses, and what he confesses, are indeed the "rock" against which the gates of hell shall not prevail. The keys of the kingdom are thus mystically given by the Lord to that body, to that Church, which faithfully confesses Him as *"Christ, the Son of the living God."* To maintain that the keys of the kingdom were directly associated with anything other than the Church's on-going fidelity to the mystical confession of Peter would be equal to abandoning both the mystery of the Church and Holy Tradition, thereby opting for a conceptual and rational formula in the way Rome, in fact, has done.

In spite of its very quick, popular appeal, the saying, *"No Pope, no Church!"* proves far too simplistic for any really thoughtful and mature approach to something as complex as the divine institution of the Church of God on earth. The Church of God is not a political entity, but, essentially, a *mystical* one. Even within the holy confines of the Church, Orthodoxy adamantly insists that it is only to the extent that the fullness of Jesus Christ as Son of the living God is actually *proclaimed* by an Orthodox bishop that bishop is himself truly an Orthodox bishop, whatever his vestments, his ecclesiastical office, his wealth, power or reputation. In much the same way Orthodoxy has always insisted that even when an Ecumenical Council reaches a decision about what is truth and what is not, such a decision, within the mystery of the Church, still remains to be proven by the Holy Spirit at work in the people of God who must accept it.

The very long struggle in regard to the Arian heresy following the Council of Nicea (325) demonstrates this very Orthodox principle. The same phenomenon was repeated after the VII. Ecumenical Council declared victory over the iconoclasts in 787, only to face a virulent resurgence of persecution ending definitively only more than a half century later in 843.

Even inspired decisions must therefore be integrated organically into the whole of Orthodoxy through the Holy Spirit, in contrast to the totalitarian nature of the Papal Church where decrees become laws immediately, even if they take on characteristics of a foreign body being grafted onto an organism attempting to reject it.

Decisions of the Seven Ecumenical Councils confirmed what had always been latently present and alive in the Church. They were thus eventually embraced and recognized because they were indeed already an integral part of the past. The condemnation of the Arian heresy was, in the end, merely a confirmation of just what St. John stated in beginning his Gospel: *"In the beginning the Word was with God and the Word was God"* (Jn 1:1).

In regard to St. Nektarios's strange vocation to sanctity in the early twentieth century, it is salutary to recall that it was not secular governments who were the demonic instruments of his persecution and worldly ruin, but rather his own jealous fellow-hierarchs, knowing he outshone them as candidate for the Patriarchal throne of Alexandria. His reputation for sanctity among the faithful caused them all to appear the very worldly bishops they were. It was therefore essential that he be maligned, his impeccable reputation sullied before the old Patriarch who, they knew, even though he actually favored Nektarios as his successor, would tolerate not the slightest whisper of moral turpitude.

Within the mystery of the Church it is therefore not necessarily always in the hierarchs themselves that the "right glory" is automatically to be found, for they too are sinners. Rather is "right glory" to be found in the confession of St. Peter alone, the confession that Jesus Christ is God. That is the "rock" upon which the Church of God is built, the guarantee of her authenticity, not the Pope of Rome.

An unfaithful bishop may of course function validly in the Church of God, thanks to God's infinite mercy and His boundless grace to those faithful believers under him. But, in those instances, it is the faith of the believers, and not the faith of the bishop that, through the Holy Spirit, gives meaning to the mystery of the Church, validating it.

The unfaithful bishop is judged, and perhaps even saved before God, by the fidelity of believers under him. By the purity of their faith, all those faithful to the mystery of St. Peter's confession render the unworthy bishop's functioning valid within the mystery of the Church. It is indeed possible to find very holy people under bishops who are heretics, just as it is possible to communicate with the Lord through sacraments given by an unworthy priest. The divine economy is vast within the mystery of the Church of God, ever proving God's great mercy to sinful men in each one's personal vocation to "right glory."

The continued manifestation of the Holy Spirit at work in the Orthodox Church through personal vocations, monastic and otherwise, continues to bestow "right glory" on an infinite variety of vocations in the world. All of these vocations, whatever they be, are Orthodox to the extent that they are lived out within the mystery of the Church, and in humble, soul-felt union with every righteous soul made perfect in faith who, since the beginning of time, has glorified God.

CHAPTER VIII

SUNDAYS OF GREAT LENT: ILLUSTRATIONS OF THE MYSTERY

Orthodoxy's eight-week preparation for Pascha consists of a week of Pre-Lent, six weeks of Lent, then Holy Week. During that time the material and the spiritual are strikingly juxtaposed with, on one hand, emphasis on the very material dietary rules held by Holy Tradition as the ideal for this time (abstinence from meat and dairy products and even oil and wine) and, on the other, the spiritual challenge of St. Ephrem's Prayer.

This prayer, so particularly associated with Great Lent and used throughout it, actually inaugurates the Great Fast each year on "Cheese-Fare Sunday," the Sunday preceding "Clean Monday," as the Greeks term the first day of Great Lent. Vespers for that day are called "Forgiveness Vespers" since priest and people join in seeking mutual forgiveness with prostrations before one another. It is the Prayer of St. Ephrem however that terminates this service. The priest, facing the holy doors with his back to the congregation, leads them in three prostrations as he prays:

O Lord and Master of my life, take from me the spirit of sloth, despondency, lust for power, and idle talk. (FIRST PROSTRATION).

MYSTERY OF THE CHURCH

But give to me Thy servant a spirit of soberness, humility, patience, and love. (SECOND PROSTRATION).

O Lord and King, grant me to see my own faults and not to judge my brother: for blessed art Thou to the ages of ages. Amen. (FINAL PROSTRATION).

St. Ephrem's prayer transcends the material and reminds the believer that the acquisition of spiritual gifts out of love for Jesus Christ and for one's neighbor is the real goal of the Great Fast, as indeed of the whole of the Christian life.

The sequence of commemorations assigned to the five Sundays of Great Lent, however, not only juxtaposes the material with the spiritual, but actually emphasizes their fusion in Orthodox life. On the first Sunday God's use of matter in the form of icons is underlined. On the second Sunday is commemorated the great teacher of Orthodoxy, St. Gregory Palamas, Archbishop of Thessaloniki, who decisively articulated Orthodoxy's stance on the sanctification of human matter through prayer, the Sacraments and love, and not through human reason and the intellect. The third Sunday holds up the necessity for man's matter to be crucified with Christ, while the fourth Sunday honors St. John of the Ladder, Abbot of Mount Sinai, who emphasized the conscious effort one must make to keep the praying soul within the body. Finally, on the Great Fast's fifth and final Sunday, a peculiarly feminine note is given with the commemoration of the very austere St. Mary of Egypt who demonstrates a remarkable and moving fusion of her body with her soul.

MYSTERY OF THE CHURCH

On the first Sunday of Great Lent each year, commonly called "Orthodoxy Sunday," the Orthodox Church glories in two quite separate and distinct victories over the iconoclasts, though a good portion of her faithful are usually under the impression that they are commemorating only one event. The first victory was the condemnation of the iconoclasts by the Seventh Ecumenical Council in 787. The second occurred in 843, following a horrendous rash of virulent persecution due to the iconoclastic Emperor Theophilus (829-842).

Launched in 726 under the Emperor Leo III the Isaurian (717-740), the sporadic iconoclast persecution of the Orthodox extended over a 116 year period, finally coming to a definitive end on the First Sunday of Great Lent in 843 when the Orthodox Empress Theodora, widow of the iconoclastic Theophilus, before the Patriarch and a large group of confessors who had suffered imprisonment, torture and disfigurement for the holy icons, venerated the icon of the Theotokos in public ceremony. In a loud and clear voice she then decreed that if anyone not kneel to the icons and kiss them in sign of veneration, then such persons were to be anathema. Publicly she besought God's forgiveness for her late husband, praying and fasting continually for this intention throughout the whole first week of the Great Fast.

The about-face of 843 allowing icons to be re-enshrined in churches and homes, and restoring their use throughout the Empire, was therefore really just a reaffirmation of the decree of 56 years before at the Seventh Ecumenical Council, convened in 787 during a respite in the iconoclastic struggle. The "Synodikon of Orthodoxy," pronounced in 843, is still solemnly read in many parishes today at the end of a procession of icon-bearing faithful honoring Theodora and the restoration of Orthodoxy on "Orthodoxy Sunday."

At the root of the iconoclastic persecution lay intellectual puritanism born of scorn for the very principle of the Incarnation itself, that is that God chose created matter for His glorification in being made flesh in Jesus Christ. What is commemorated on this first Sunday of Lent therefore is the on-going demonstration, through icons, that God manifests Himself to the world through created matter: He is indeed a God of the Incarnation who still does not disdain using created matter to express His glory.

The image presented in an icon is, as it were, a fixed and prayerful memory, a veritable presence rising heavenward to what is represented. Thereby does that presence become more accessible on earth, just as a photograph may render those who are long dead present to those who love them.

In many respects the cult of the icon is moreover interchangeable with the cult of relics. In both cases matter is recognized as being able to communicate the power of God. Veneration shown them, whether through prostrations before God's presence in them, candles lighted before them, or incense, hymns and processions offered in their honor, all typify the cult normally surrounding both icons and relics among the Orthodox.

Relics of course constitute the matter that actually made up the saint's body. Imbued with divine energies they may communicate God's presence. Yet icons also, in some cases, seem to take on a mysterious life of their own. Hidden, and often miracle-working icons, may be made manifest after a dream or divine revelation to some pious person, just as the location of lost relics may also be made known by divine revelation. Certainly Holy Tradition proves both icons and relics to be mighty Orthodox witnesses in the service of God. Both confirm the penetration of the mystery of the church's mystical life into the material, daily flesh and blood existence of the faithful.

The iconoclasts, who tortured, imprisoned, martyred and maimed so many of the Orthodox, did approach God from an intellectual and anti-incarnational point of view. The disincarnate nature of iconoclasm might be likened to the rationalistic, masculine principle trying to triumph over the more basic and integrated feminine principle. In Orthodoxy there must always be a healthy balance between these two natures. By the iconoclasts' intellectual stance against the sanctification of matter their faith became unbalanced and sectarian. Like modern Protestants, the iconoclasts reasoned that God, being spiritual, does not need matter to show forth His glory. They therefore tried to suppress the most basic human instinct by which one treasures images of what one loves.

Though theoretically forbidden in Judaism and Islam, the use and love of images is, in fact, almost universal. Even non-Christians cherish the photographs of those they love, placing them in a place of honor in their most intimate surroundings, reaching out to touch, or even to kiss them. How much more then should baptized Christians honor images of their Lord and God, Jesus Christ, of his holy and ever-virgin Mother, and of His saints who constitute the elders of that great family who have "put on Christ" in baptism?

Paradoxically, in the iconoclastic controversy, icons were defended by the most austere of Christians, the monastics. They who had renounced all excessive use of matter in their own lives, be it food, drink or raiment, and, at times, even the most simple shelter to protect them from the elements, vehemently insisted that the use of icons to proclaim God's glory was a matter of faith, essential to the spiritual struggle of man. On the other hand, the iconoclastic party was led by Emperors with their armies, plus politically ambitious bishops and patriarchs, all of whose lives were made pleasant by an abundance of food, drink, raiment and sumptuous palaces.

Thanks to their powerful positions in the Empire, the iconoclasts, at the end of 116 years of intermittent persecution, had effected a veritable purge of icons throughout the Byzantine Empire. This mass destruction of images was so thorough-going that icons dating prior to 843 are exceedingly rare today and seen only in a few centers, such as St. Catherine's monastery on Mt. Sinai, which escaped Byzantine persecution.

The triumph of the "right glory" of Orthodoxy over the iconoclasts was therefore of fundamental importance in according matter its rightful place in the life of an Orthodox Christian. Matter, like all of God's creation, exists to serve Him. Consecrated to God, it has the potential for communicating God's presence to man. Himself submitted to the Creator, the Orthodox believer is drawn not only to others who are also submitted to God, but also to matter that gives off the "right glory" of God as icons and relics sometimes do.

The contrast is strong, however, between what is submitted to God and what is not. Chief rebel against any submission to God is of course the Prince of this world, who scorns anything submitted to God, be it beings, or inert matter, such as icons and relics. Both are equally hated and willed to destruction by the demonic powers. Thus only can be explained the terrible persecution suffered by the Orthodox from the iconoclasts. In our own century we have seen similar demonic hatred destroy relics, icons and churches by God-hating political regimes, along with the slaughter of countless martyrs.

ii

Just as the First Sunday of Great Lent affirms the role of matter in the manifestation of God's glory, the Second Sunday's commemoration of the great Metropolitan of Thessaloniki, St. Gregory Palamas (1296-1359) emphasizes how flesh and blood can be illuminated by the Uncreated Light of God. The Orthodox Church venerates Gregory Palamas for having saved Orthodoxy from the West's delusions of Renaissance humanism wherein, as demonstrated by St. Thomas Aquinas, belief in God is approached through man's reason, rather than through the sacraments, through prayer and love. St. Gregory Palamas's teaching merely confirmed these basic, Biblical truths preserved by the monks who knew them through their unceasing prayer of the heart, known as the "hesychist" tradition.

Indeed, the unbroken eastern monastic tradition defended by Gregory Palamas was the Biblical tradition. Both maintained that the goal and end of the Christian life is that of *theosis*, that is of truly becoming sons of God in the flesh, as taught in the Gospel of St. John. Not only does the idea of theosis confirm the clear Gospel teaching that Jesus Christ came to earth that we might become, through Him, sons of God: *"as many as received him, to them gave he power to become the sons of God, even to them that believe on his name"* (Jn 1:12), but also St. Paul's teaching that Christians are destined to become *"joint-heirs with Christ"* (Rom 8: 17) in the Kingdom of the Holy Trinity.

The possibility that this basic apostolic truth might be true-- that is that we can become the sons of God--has naturally aroused the ire of the Enemy. The Roman Church however has blindly persisted in maintaining that St. Gregory Palamas's teaching was not basic Christianity at all, but rather some rarefied quasi-heretical doctrine called "Palamism," whereby the saint defended unkept monks who thought that by incessant prayer one could take on the nature of God Himself. The suppression of the commemoration of St. Gregory Palamas by Roman's "eastern rite" Melchite Church confirms how deeply the Roman Church finds this great Orthodox father's "right glory" inimical to her deeply entrenched rationalistic stance.

Orthodoxy's "right glory" is no doubt in no small measure derived from St. Gregory Palamas's insistence upon the difference between the "energies" of God and the "essence" of God, something unheard of in the West. Orthodoxy insists that the energies of God, through the Holy Spirit, are present everywhere and fill all creation, whereas the essence of God, what He himself really is, and what distinguishes Him from His creation, is completely *other*. What is created remains created and can never partake of the *essence* of the Uncreated--in which case it would indeed become God. Yet it can, nonetheless, partake of the divine *energies* of God which, like rays, eternally emanate from His unknowable, unfathomable and ineffable uncreated essence. These energies are always available to man. By becoming increasingly imbued with them man becomes more God-like even though, quite obviously, he can never be God.

Compared with the rationalist western approach to God where every movement, every twinge of grace is defined, Orthodoxy's distinction between the essence and the energies of God greatly simplifies the relationship between God and man. For the Orthodox, grace, like any other good thing that comes from God, is simply a manifestation of the divine energies, not something set apart and classified as to type, kind and origin, as is done in the West. Grace is but one among the countless manifestations of the energies of God at work in the world: the Sacraments, human fidelity and sacrifice, the beauty of God's creation, and any other good thing.

Orthodox cosmology indeed allows only two distinctions: the uncreated Creator, Almighty God himself, and His creation--that is, everything else, visible and invisible, including angels or demons. Orthodoxy has no place for, and no patience with, what is commonly called the "supernatural." That is why the peculiarly western distinction between "supernatural grace" and "natural grace" is totally meaningless for the Orthodox mind. As for grace itself, the West's attempt to situate it somewhere below God, but above man, seems to the Orthodox extremely complicated and a fabrication of human reasoning by western clerics. It is totally unfounded in Orthodox's experience of God within Holy Tradition.

Indeed, by rejecting Orthodoxy's basic and very simple distinction between God's eternally incommunicable and uncreated essence, and His constantly communicable energies, continually at work in the world, Western

MYSTERY OF THE CHURCH

Christianity split the wholeness of the cosmos. For the Orthodox all is contained in the two categories of "Creator" and "created." Of what value then are dreamed-up categories distinguishing "natural" and "supernatural"? The divine energies allow man that "great freedom" which is Orthodoxy, permitting him to seek God in everything around him without having to define how that is possible, or what sort of grace might, in such circumstances, be necessary to allow man to experience God.

It was in using rationalistic terms that the Western Church paved the way for the Protestant onslaught. Martin Luther saw a "conflict" between "faith" and "works," opposing one against the other, even to the extent of regretting, it is said, the admission of the Epistle of St. James to the Canon of Holy Scriptures since that first Bishop of Jerusalem and brother of the Lord insisted that "*faith without works is dead*" (Jas 2:20). Arguments distinguishing between grace and nature-- and, subsequently, defining what the sacraments are and are not--all these things have no meaning in Orthodoxy. Belief in the divine energies encompasses everything touching upon man's relationship with God as well as his relationship with his brothers.

Emanating from God, the divine energies are poured out on all creation through the Holy Spirit. All that is good comes from them. A man who loves God will make an active effort to partake of the divine energies through prayer, through the sacraments, through his love of God and his brother. Thus does the believer, if his love for God be above all things, strive to become ever more filled with the power and presence of God through the divine energies, thereby "*acquiring the Holy Spirit*" as St. Seraphim of Sarov urged us to do. St. Gregory Palamas's teaching was moreover perfectly illustrated by St. Seraphim's illumination in the Holy Spirit before his disciple

v

The veneration of the cross on the Third Sunday of Great Lent cuts the Great Fast into two parts. After we have been presented, on the first Sunday, with the truth that God uses created matter for His glory, we are reminded on the Second Sunday that that first truth must be integrated into our flesh and blood through prayer and loving cooperation with the divine energies. Firmly set on the road to sanctification of our flesh and blood by the first two Sundays, the Third Sunday confronts us with the stark reality to which our flesh and blood are being led: the cross of God incarnate, crucified and resurrected.

For Christianity the cross is *reality*. It is an image of human destiny in this world: death. Nor is it by any means representative only of that final door through which we must all pass. The cross also represents each of those little deaths we must embrace day by day, hour by hour, and minute by minute as, out of love for Christ, we take up our cross to follow Him and be daily crucified with Him.

The repeated singing of the troparion for the Cross-- *"Save O Lord thy people, and bless thine inheritance! [...] Preserve thy habitation by thy cross!"* -- has an on-going validity for Orthodox Christians year after year. Being, as they are, the bearers of the fullness of the Resurrected Christ, they know that they can only expect the ill-will of the Enemy of the race of men to rain down upon them. It is against him

111

that they pray to be preserved. Moreover since the original Greek text of this troparion states: "*Grant victory to thy kings against the Enemy!*" this petition can, mystically at least, actually still be validly employed at the parish level since every believer is a "king" and is indeed fully engaged in an on-going battle with the Enemy of the race for the salvation of his soul.

It is to be regretted that translators have made free with this troparion, turning it into a battle-cry to give a collective "Orthodox people" victory over all their enemies. For centuries some ethnic Orthodox have drawn from this troparion a political justification for warring against their non-Orthodox neighbors. The sense of every individual Christian soul's being engaged in a mystical struggle against the demonic is thereby not only lost, but perverted into a political statement for a collectivity.

On this Third Sunday believers also venerate the Cross as the great Christian reality, singing, "*Lord, thy Cross do we venerate! And we do glorify thy holy Resurrection!*" The Passion and the Resurrection are thus fused together and kept in balance in the very best Orthodox tradition, never allowing the sufferings of Christ to be separated from the miracle of His Resurrection. (Here again one regrets those translations reading: "*Before thy Cross we bow down in worship,*" which makes it far more difficult to convince the non-Orthodox that the Orthodox worship God alone, and that devotion to saints, icons and relics in holy Orthodoxy is not worship, but veneration!)

MYSTERY OF THE CHURCH

vi

On the Fourth Sunday of Great Lent, St. John Climacus, author of *The Ladder of the Divine Ascent*, is commemorated. In this essentially monastic manual on asceticism, the great Abbot of the monastery on Mt. Sinai left us a detailed series of instructions, both practical and mystical, on how monks, to whom it was addressed, are to take up the cross and follow Jesus Christ as they try to mount the "ladder of divine ascent."

Understanding the unity of all God's creation, St. John teaches that the monk truly seeking *theosis*, that is becoming a son of God, must learn above all else to keep his soul *within* his body when he prays. He must not allow it to go wandering off into fantasized celestial places.

The transformation of the matter of our bodies through ascetic practices is therefore neither the end nor the goal of the quest. Rather is the goal that of keeping the soul contained within the body as it rises to God in prayer. Thereby alone may the body again become inextricably joined to the soul as it strives towards transfiguration, thus ultimately healing the basic psychic split between flesh and spirit, so deeply embedded in fallen man.

Since leaving the body behind would only further increase fallen man's psychic split between matter and spirit, anyone seeking union with God should strive to achieve sanctification within the created matter given us by God: the human body. St. John of the Ladder's admonition to keep our souls within our bodies when we pray is therefore basic both to an Orthodox understanding of prayer according to Holy Tradition, as well as to the Church's experience of the nature of fallen man.

MYSTERY OF THE CHURCH

St. John of the Ladder's admonitions about fusing soul and body together lead to the commemoration of St. Mary of Egypt on the fifth and final Sunday of Great Lent. She indeed is a glowing example of how the divine energies of God transfigured flesh and blood, resulting from her living out the admonition of St. John to keep the soul *within* the body whenever one prays.

Mary of Egypt's example also illumines in a quite remarkable way what actually happens whenever a soul rises above the temptation of thinking of the Church as something other than oneself, that is, something other than one's own personal life in Jesus Christ, hidden in the depths of the divine economy, through the Holy Spirit. For though outwardly living totally apart from the life of her fellow-Christians for 47 years, St. Mary was actually situated at the very heart of the mystery of the Church. Through bitter spiritual struggles, she probably, more than any hierarch of the time, was not only maintaining the Faith of the Church, but offering the world an incarnation of the power of Christ to save fallen man.

Certainly Father Zossima, the abbot who discovered her and gave her Holy Communion, considered her his superior. Every Orthodox hierarch who venerates her witness on the Fifth Sunday of Great Lent annually recognizes in her example a profound truth. Though prior to her conversion her respect for the Christian faith in which she had been baptized had been so slight that she had no qualms about joining a boatload of Christian pilgrims to Jerusalem to ply her trade as a prostitute en route, through the great mercy of God's divine economy she was thereby to encounter an icon of the Godbirthgiver at the door of the Holy Sepulcher in Jerusalem.

MYSTERY OF THE CHURCH

This would change her heart and lead her to her long, solitary repentance, totally unknown to the world until, 47 years later, she was discovered by Fr. Zossima.

St. Mary of Egypt's hidden witness was sent by God to confound Fr. Zossima who had pridefully gone out of his monastery into the desert wondering if there were anyone who matched him in his Lenten asceticism. The Holy Mother astounded him when, without even thinking of what she was doing, she crossed the little stream separating them by walking on its waters. Fr. Zossima was also humbled again when he saw her suspended above the ground as she raised her hands to pray for the Church and for the world.

Like the proud Fr. Zossima, all Orthodox Christians are invited on the Fifth Sunday of Great Lent to learn the great lesson held daily before them by St. Ephrem's Prayer and exemplified by their Holy Mother, Mary of Egypt: the purging of sloth, despondence, lust for power and idle talk that one may acquire the spirit of soberness, humility, patience and love. Only thus does one come to know one's own faults and not judge one's brother.

The mystery of St. Mary of Egypt's witness allows us therefore not only to take a first step towards our grasp of the mystery of Christian life, but also a first step towards understanding the ineffable mystery of the Church at work in the fallen world.

CHAPTER IX

SUPREME IMAGE OF THE MYSTERY:
BRIDEGROOM MATINS

Beginning Palm Sunday evening, and continuing the three following evenings of "Great Week" -- as Holy Week is called in Greek--, Orthodox Christians are invited to worship Jesus Christ as the Divine Bridegroom of the Church. This service presents Him not only as the Bridegroom of the Church, but, at the same time, as the personal Bridegroom of the soul of every believer.

The first Bridegroom Matins, that for Monday, sung on Palm Sunday evening by anticipation, is highly dramatic. Mounted with lighted candles and borne aloft by the priest, the icon of the Bridegroom, accompanied by smoking censer and lights, emerges from inside the altar and is carried in procession around the darkened church, then set up for veneration by the faithful until Holy Thursday.

If one thinks that such an icon should show a victorious Christ in majesty, its reality proves shocking. Never has a Bridegroom looked less comely, fulfilling the prophecy of Isaiah:

> "[...] *he hath no form nor comeliness; and when we shall see him, there is no beauty that we should desire him. He is despised and rejected of men; a man of sorrows, and acquainted with grief.*" (Isa 53:2-3).

MYSTERY OF THE CHURCH

Indeed, what we see is the image of the humiliated, flagellated Christ as He appeared before Pilate, bleeding, crowned with thorns. For the western observer it appears a Byzantine rendering of the familiar *"Ecce homo,"* so favored by Italian masters.

Prior to the dramatic entrance of the icon, and immediately following Matins' opening Six Psalms, four verses have been intoned by the priest, each verse answered by three very solemn Alleluias. All four verses express the sorrowing awe with which the Church of God now confronts the reality of a dark world which rejected, and still rejects her Bridegroom.

The first verse, *"My spirit seeks Thee early in the night watches, for Thy commandments are a light on the earth,"* speaks both for the Church as the Bride of Christ who seeks the Beloved, as also for every soul who also seeks in Him, the only Light holding good against the reign of death in this world. The first set of three mournful and melismatically prolonged Alleluias then resounds, after which the priest intones an admonishment to those who are earth-bound and do not seek the Light of the Bridegroom: *"Learn righteousness, ye that dwell upon the earth."*

Following the prolonged triple Alleluia, the third verse proves the most powerful yet, evoking as it does the judgement of the world by fire. *"Jealousy shall seize upon an untaught people and fire shall devour the adversaries."* In awed assent before this image of fiery destruction, the Church, the Bride of Christ, replies once again with her three mournful Alleluias.

The fourth verse, however, is the strongest, born of the horror of the abyss the Church beholds between the image of the scourged Jesus of Nazareth and the glory of this world. It matters little whether that glory be the imperial glory of a Roman Emperor such as Tiberius Caesar, under whose authority Pontius Pilate ordered the Lord's flagellation and subsequent humiliation at the hands of crude, sadistic Roman soldiers, or the flashy, tawdry glory of media hype for today's latest sex-and-drug-addicted pop star. *"Bring more evils upon them, O Lord, bring more evils upon those who are glorious upon the earth,"* the Church cries out, confronted with the scandal of her humiliated Lord and Bridegroom, the Creator of all things, reduced to the role of the suffering servant. The solemnity of this terrible verse is enhanced once again by the closing sorrowful and prolonged three-fold Alleluia.

One must of course be mindful of the unique context in which all of this takes place. The end of the eight weeks of the Great Fast is at hand. The Church, scandalized by the gross and callous injustice towards her scourged young Bridegroom, cries out against the wickedness of fallen men who perpetrated the monstrosity of deicide, and who would, she knows, repeat it all again. Even more disquieting, however, is the fact that those faithful to the Bridegroom may also be called upon to follow His example, just as His Bride, the Church, has so often been called upon to do. Across twenty centuries of Christian history, one can only wonder how many times, during periods of persecution, tears of the threatened faithful have accompanied these sorrowful Alleluias.

The hymn, *"Behold! the Bridegroom cometh,"* which so dramatically illustrates the parable of the wise and foolish virgins with its admonishment to keep watchful vigil and not miss His coming, accompanies the initial appearance of the

118

icon the first evening and is sung three times. The three-fold singing of this hymn is also repeated at each of the Bridegroom Matins.

> *Behold! the Bridegroom cometh, in the middle of the night:*
> *Blessed is the servant whom he shall find watching!*
> *Unworthy he whom He shall find, slothful and heedless!*
> *Watch therefore O my soul,*
> *Lest thou be overcome by sleep;*
> *Lest thou be given over unto death;*
> *Lest thou find the kingdom fast closed to thee!*
> *Arouse thyself therefore and cry aloud:*
> *Holy! Holy! Holy! is the Lord of hosts!*

Setting up the icon on that first evening evokes the presence of the humiliated Bridegroom in the midst of His fasting faithful as Pascha approaches. Candle stands placed near the icon are kept aflame with candles offered by the worshippers who, as they enter the church during those first days of Holy Week, venerate the icon of the Bridegroom with prostrations, kisses, prayers and tears of love.

For lovers of God, Bridegroom Matins proves to be a service of terrible, troubling beauty. The Bridegroom of the Church is openly revealed not as a Spouse on whom one can rely for escaping judgment and unlawful execution at the hands of wicked men, but rather as One subject to all the powers of the Prince of this world that conspired together to humiliate and slay Him, the Lord of Glory.

Yet, at the same time, the Church keeps a very balanced perspective in contemplating this horror. She knows *who* the Bridegroom is, for *"all things were made by him; and without him was not any thing made that was made"* (Jn 1:3). She knows also that it is by the Bridegroom that the world will be judged, both by the glory of His Transfiguration and Resurrection, and by the injustice of His humiliation and death.

It is for this reason that on Holy Saturday morning at the beginning of the Divine Liturgy of St. Basil, the Priest will emerge from the holy doors, scattering bay leaves and inviting the slumbering Bridegroom to break God's long silence: *"Rise up, O God, and judge thou the earth!"* Indeed, the earth has been judged by its action of putting the Lord of Glory to death, and shall continue to be judged by this until the end of time.

ii

The cult of the Bridegroom, one of the most mysterious and profound in Orthodoxy, is rooted in an essential mystery. The Church, through her devotion to the flagellated Divine Bridegroom, is called upon to function as a Bride worthy of such a Spouse. Believers who are persecuted continue to find consolation and courage in uniting themselves to the sufferings of the Bridegroom, the object of their hearts' true love.

Such an orientation of longing for, even evoking the advent of the Bridegroom with its subsequent end of the age is, of course, ancient. In the *Didache*, going back to the second century, the Eucharistic prayer ended with the petition, "*Let grace come, and let this world pass away!*" The Lord's cry at the very end of the book of Revelation, "*Surely I come quickly!*" (Rev 22:20) is answered by the urgent assent of the Beloved John: "*Even so, come, Lord Jesus!*" (Rev 22:20). This is the cry which has ever not only announced the imminent return of the Bridegroom with His judgement, but which actually, across the centuries, continues to be the Church's cry, summoning Him to return to reclaim what is rightfully His.

We see then that for all of the glory of Orthodoxy's exulting in the transfiguration of matter throughout Great Lent, it all leads in the end to this image of the humiliated Bridegroom. This is the final lesson as the Church prepares for the unspeakable joy of the Pascal feast. It is this that lies hidden in her heart as her most intimate conjugal secret. The terrible crown of humiliation placed on the head of Him, the Son of the pure Virgin, born of immaculate, innocent matter, stands before his Bride, judged by the world. Scourged and scoffingly wrapped in a purple robe of shame, holding a reed as a mock scepter in bound hands, His face stained from the spittle and buffetings of rough Roman soldiers, the blood that redeems the world trickling down from His thorn-pierced brow: this is the image of absolute reality He offers His Bride and, through her, to the world. In accord with the prophecy of Isaiah, "*the Lord hath laid on him the iniquity of us all*" (Is 53:6), and we, mortal men, are given to behold utter innocence crowned with thorns by the mighty Roman empire.

Only to the extent that her Bridegroom's humility becomes her own is the Bride truly worthy of such a Bridegroom, however. Unjust suffering and persecution must often also be her lot. Yet with what joy shall His bride be singing, in less than a week's time, her irrepressible victory: *"Christ is risen from the dead, having trampled death by death!"*

For the pious soul, sensitive to the mystery of the divine economy in the Incarnation, the icon of the thorn-crowned, scourged Bridegroom, pledged not only to crucifixion, but also to Resurrection after He has harrowed Hades, does bear witness to the balance within Orthodoxy between His Passion and the "right glory" He came to show us. This is the glory spoken of at the Transfiguration on Mt. Tabor before Peter, James and John, the glory to which Moses and Elijah were privy and bore witness as they conversed of the *"coming decease"* of the only-begotten Son and Word of God. Within the unfathomable depths of the mystery of the Church, the sorrowing Bridegroom is indeed also the sorrowing glory of the Bride of Christ. His triumphs over the worst that the Enemy can put forward are also hers.

Such a vision of the Church, of course, is totally abhorrent to the Prince of darkness who ever wishes to prevail against the Bridegroom. As Prince of this world, Satan is jealous of anything threatening his sovereignty in his earthly princedom. He would, if it were allowed him, become the only power at work in it. With the Orthodox Church assuring, as it does, the dynamism of the Holy Trinity at work in this world of which he is the Prince, the illusion of absolute power and irremediable sovereignty he would perpetuate in the minds of the human race is constantly being challenged.

An incident occurring during the Soviet regime has left us with the story of how the Resurrection of Jesus Christ still has the power to overcome the gloom and despair of the Prince of darkness and death. In a village where the church had not been reopened, the old priest badgered the local committee into reluctantly agreeing to allow him to celebrate the Pascal Liturgy that year. They had not anticipated, however, that on Holy Saturday morning the tiny village would start filling up with hundreds upon hundreds of worshippers coming from miles around, expectantly gathering for the midnight service. Quickly repenting of their weakness, the committee called for the priest and immediately rescinded their permission. They would immediately announce to the ever-increasing crowd that the service had been canceled and that they should all go home peacefully.

But even as they spoke the press of people was becoming ever greater and more insistent, so that a sort of panic seized the committee as they pondered what the reaction might be to their announcement. The old priest therefore had no difficulty in persuading them that, since it would be good politics not to incite a riot, a brief word from him might perhaps help. They agree, but on condition that it be very brief. He assured them that he literally had only one statement to make, nothing more, and promised them that afterwards, moreover, the crowd would all disperse peacefully.

Proudly turning up the village's hyper-efficient loudspeaker system to its highest decibel, the committee chairman officiously announced that there would be no service that evening but that, before they all returned home, the priest had a word for them. Gripping the microphone with his left hand, and with eyes blazing, the old priest deliberately raised his right hand to his forehead to sign the cross as he shouted with a vigorous, defiant joy into the microphone: "*Christ is risen!*" From every corner, from every throat, and, as it were from one burning defiance of heart and soul, the cry of the Orthodox faithful roared back, taunting the dark powers of hell and death without the slightest hesitation: *"Indeed He's risen!"* Then they all went home in peace.

Thus was the high feast of the Lamb kept that year in one tiny village in atheist Russia. The Resurrection of Jesus Christ was by no means a thing of the past. Its power could still dispel the darkness, gloom and despair of Satan and his reign of death in the Union of Soviet Socialist Republics.

iii

The fall of Constantinople to the Turks in 1453 effectively meant that the Eastern--and Orthodox--Empire was taken over by Islam. It offered the Western world a prominent image of on-going Christian humiliation, a jarring contrast to the surging, harmonious architecture so confidently rising to replace the venerable old St. Peter's in Rome, heritage of less enlightened days. But as one tired to sustain the myth of the "progress" of humankind, promised by the humanist Renaissance and espoused by a burgeoning Vatican, how annoyingly awkward it was for the highly visible Hagia Sophia to be converted into a mosque! The contrast between vanquished Orthodoxy and Rome's militant church with the Pope as the supreme pontiff of the organized Kingdom of God on earth was impressive. Mind-sets were formed at that time that still prevail in the West, bolstered by subsequent centuries of repeated innuendoes concerning Orthodoxy's basic lacks, inadequacies, and backwardness.

Yet, in a very real sense, the cult of the humiliated Bridegroom does evoke, more than anything else, the image of an humiliated Bride, not a triumphant one, *"glorious upon the earth,"* as is St. Peter's of Rome with all its Renaissance glory. The cult of the Bridegroom in any case does provide consolation for the Orthodox who, while regretting the loss of Constantinople in 1453, must still also humbly recall that only months before that fall, the act of union with Rome had been solemnly read out in Hagia Sophia, violating Holy Orthodoxy and betraying the mystery of the Church.

The liturgical genius of transforming the Old Testament prophecy of the Suffering Servant-- *"he was wounded for our transgressions, he was bruised for our iniquities: the chastisement of our peace was upon him; and with his stripes we are healed"* (Is 53:5)--into the Bridegroom of the Church is, in any case, remarkable in its all-encompassing fusion. Deeply integrated into the whole mystique of the first services of Holy Week, it clearly points to Him as the Beloved of the believer's own soul. This latter orientation is carried to ineffable heights in the thrice-sung Exposteilarion which, as it were, crowns Bridegroom Matins. The soul, smitten with love for the Beloved, and urgently seeking greater intimacy still, cries out in the words of Romanos Melodos:

> *Thy bridal chamber I see, my Saviour,*
> *And it is adorned.*
> *Yet no wedding garment have I*
> *That I might enter therein!*
> *Make radiant the vesture of my soul,*
> *O Giver of Light, and save me!*

It is through such intimate love for the Bridegroom that the Holy Spirit, Who is *"present in all places"* and *"filleth all things,"* strives to woo the hearts of men back to the Kingdom. *"The Spirit itself maketh intercession for us with groanings which cannot be uttered"* (Rom 8:26), the Apostle observes, and love of the Bridegroom does become for the believer a veritable recovery of that lost Paradise from which our first ancestors fell. This regained Paradise is found only in the New Adam, Jesus Christ, the flagellated Bridegroom, given the world through the new Eve, Mary.

In Him, the Lamb slain from the foundation of the world and the Church's Bridegroom, is indeed the experience of heaven on earth, discovered not only in Hagia Sophia by Prince Vladimir's emissaries, but by all who, in approaching His Bride in faith, love and fear of God, seek Him and Him alone. For bodiless heavenly powers with swords of fire may well guard the Paradise which is the fullness of Christ preserved for mankind in the Orthodox Church, but that fullness is nonetheless available and freely given to those who seek Him with love. Indeed, all the glory He shared with the Father before the world began is given them, as is also the underlying sorrow, shame and suffering of His sublime Passion through which Paradise was restored. To them it is given, as to St. Paul, to *"make up what is lacking in the afflictions of Christ"* (Col 1:24).

Christians who in embarrassment turn away from the mystery of the flagellated Bridegroom of course are turning away from the divine economy of God of which they, as creatures of God, are a part. They allow themselves to start reasoning that it is they themselves who command the Church of God, forgetting that God alone commands all things, including His Church. Firmly entrenched behind their conceptual barriers, such Christians may even become convinced that it is given them to impose Paradise on earth. Such is the perennial temptation of the Pharisee, of the Inquisitor, of all religious persecutors, as well as of those pontiffs who speak of the Church's having it within its power to bring peace to this world of which, alas! Satan is Prince.

To pure hearts alone is given an experience of the mystery of the Church as revealed by the scourged Bridegroom. Thus is explained the ascetical attempt by the pious Orthodox soul inspired by the Holy Spirit to purify the heart, for the Lord promised: *"blessed are the pure in heart, for they shall see God"* (Mat 5:8).

Yet, in the end, we know, according to the promise of the Bridegroom and mystic Lamb, the frustrated Enemy is destined finally to be foiled. The promise of Jesus Christ that the gates of hell shall not prevail against the One, Holy, Catholic and Apostolic Church still stands. The Orthodox Christian ever bears in his heart the promise: *"Heaven and earth shall pass away, but my words shall not pass away"* (Mat 24:35).

iv

The experience of the mystery of the Church is therefore not to be found in man's ideas or theories, but rather in the heart that is united to the divine Bridegroom. For the heart is the seat of the human person in Judo-Christian tradition. In the heart is rooted the sanctification of the flesh and blood of believers by Jesus Christ through the power of the Holy Spirit. This sanctification has as many forms as there are sanctified believers, each one unique, yet still a continuation of the one Incarnation of God in Christ, within the mystery of the Church. A saint shows forth the "right glory" of Orthodoxy, for he is indeed planted upon the rock of St. Peter's confession that Jesus is the Christ, the Son of the Living God. Fixed upon that rock, the saints, martyrs and confessors for Orthodoxy, even in our own times, have continued to bear witness that they are united to the divine Bridegroom during, as well as after, their lifetime on this earth.

Every Orthodox communicant participating sincerely in the Communion prayers before approaching the Holy Sacrament prepares his heart for sanctification by laying aside all personal concepts of glory in this world, including his conceptualizations of God and of the mystery of the Church. These prayers required that he assume the stance of the dying, penitent thief, crucified and in agony beside the Lord. It was to this thief, nonetheless, that it was given to enter into Paradise with Him the same day. Every faithful soul who approaches the holy chalice is called upon therefore to put off all reasoning and to pray with his heart alone: "*I will not give Thee the kiss of Judas, but with the thief will I confess Thee: Remember me, O Lord, when Thou comest into Thy kingdom!*"

That such intimacy with a crucified criminal should be so idealized in an Orthodox liturgical text is, of course, in perfect accord with the "right glory" of the Bridegroom. It is no wonder that so many non-Orthodox are struck by surprise when they hear the Orthodox make such pointed references to Judas and the dying thief as they pray the pre-Communion prayers, as it were, rejecting the one and accepting the other as a sort of role-model for Christian perfection.

MYSTERY OF THE CHURCH

Yet it is only when assuming the stance of the thief and making his prayer one's own that the believer can put aside his conceptualizations as he approaches the holy chalice. In that moment of supreme, absolute reality, the believer's heart must be free to reach out to the Bridegroom with naught but love, and love for naught, save for Him alone. That he, the ever-unworthy believer, has dared step forward to partake of that unspeakable Eternal Life flowing from the chalice, can never stem from his having overcome his sense of unworthiness, which can only leave him in despair, but rather from an even greater sense of God's great and unfathomable mercy to him. As a pre-communion prayer of St. Basil the Great states so perceptively:

I know, O Lord, that I partake unworthily of Thy pure Body and of Thy precious Blood, and am guilty, and eat and drink condemnation to myself, not discerning thy Body and Blood, my Christ and my God: yet emboldened by Thy lovingkindness I come to Thee, who has said, He that eateth my Flesh and drinketh my Blood, abideth in me and I in him. Be pitiful, therefore, O Lord, and put me not to rebuke, a sinner, but deal with me according to Thy mercy.

Neither intelligence, reason, learning, nor logic allows man entry into the depths of the mystery of the Body and Blood of the Lamb anymore than they allow him into the mystery of the Church. The mysteries of Christ lie forever beyond the human mind but are accessible to him who humbly prays from the heart, as did the dying thief:

MYSTERY OF THE CHURCH

"Remember me, O Lord, when Thou comest into Thy Kingdom."

By the Lord's merciful memory of each believer piously approaching the holy chalice with repentance in his heart and with the words of the dying thief on his impure lips, he may still, like the thief, also be received "today" into the Paradise of Christ our God. In that moment, in the utter humility of his heart and soul and mind, he is completely at one with the mystery of the Church of God through the Holy Spirit. Indeed, he has become an incarnation of the "right glory" of the Father, so scandalously and paradoxically revealed to the world at the beginning of Holy Week by the thorn-crowned and scourged Bridegroom.

CHAPTER X

THE MOST HOLY GODBIRTHGIVER, PROTECTRESS AND PLEDGE OF THE MYSTERY

The most holy Birthgiver of God and ever-virgin Mary, sovereign Lady of all Christian souls, not only protects the mystery of the Church but, in a very real sense, is the veritable incarnation of that mystery. Being the eternal incarnation of the mystery, she is thereby the eternal gage offered by the race of men to God. Regularly addressed by the Orthodox as *"Protectress of Christians, who cannot be put to shame,"* she, the Godbirthgiver, is indeed *"the most constant Mediation unto the Creator"* for our fallen race.

In a troparion sung for Christmas Vespers, the Orthodox marvel at offerings made to the new-born Christ: the star given by the heavens, the gifts of the Magi, the wonder of the shepherds, and the cave given by the earth. The text then poses the rhetorical question, *"What shall we offer Thee, O Christ, who for our sakes hast appeared on earth as man?"* and, representing the human race, the Orthodox confidently sing in reply: *"We offer thee a Virgin Mother."*

The physical presence of the Godbirthgiver in the midst of the apostles as they kept prayerful vigil awaiting the outpouring of the Holy Spirit on the day of Pentecost (Acts 1:14), underlines the powerful, silent role the holy Godbirthgiver indeed played, from the beginning, in the mystery of the Church of God. Still filled with the power of the Holy Spirit, Who continually dwells in her, she continues to this day to play her silent role in the midst of those who, loving her Son, keep fervent vigil, awaiting, from generation to generation, the outpouring of the Holy Spirit on the Church. A willing receptacle for the Incarnation of the Second Person of the Holy Trinity, she thereby became an eternally consecrated vessel from which the saving action of the Spirit would continue to be poured out on the world.

In accord with the divine economy, the salvation of the human race was indeed made to hang upon the response of a single member of that race. Her assent to the Archangel Gabriel at the Annunciation-- *"Behold the handmaid of the Lord; be it unto me according to thy word"* (Lk 1:38)--went far beyond a one-time assent, however. Offered mystically on behalf of the whole race of men and making possible the eternal designs of the Master of Creation, it is an eternal assent.

Her answer to God was therefore, and still is, a valid answer for all men. Moreover, since the divine economy wills that God continue to be incarnate within the plenitude of our own human freedom, with no violation of our own human will, her answer shall remain valid as long as the race endures. In demonstrating such divine wisdom through her response to God, the most holy Godbirthgiver became the prototype for every Christian soul, male or female. Is the universal vocation of all Christians not her own, that is bringing forth Christ from their flesh that men may see Him and glorify the Father?

The original Greek text of the creed of Nicea is surprisingly explicit regarding the indispensable and freely played role of the Holy Virgin in bringing about the Incarnation. Jesus Christ is there proclaimed to have been "*incarnate by the Holy Spirit __AND__ the Virgin Mary*," rather than "*__OF__ the Virgin Mary*." Her very human role therefore was an active, and not a passive one. It was equal in importance to the divine role played by the Holy Spirit.

Unfortunately, when the Greek text passed into Latin, this basic truth got lost through a distortion in translation. The Greek word "*kai*" ("*and*") was not rendered by the Latin "*et*" meaning "*and*," but rather by the Latin "*ex*," meaning "*from*" or "*of*." Whether this mistranslation came about deliberately, or through some negligent copyist's error--the difference between "et" and "ex" is only one letter--the result was theologically disastrous. The Latin Creed states that the Godbirthgiver's role in the Incarnation was passive, not active. Thus, according to the Latin Creed Jesus Christ was "*incarnate by the Holy Spirit __OF__ the Virgin Mary*" instead of "*__AND__ the Virgin Mary*" as in the Greek text.

The Latin text being the basis for all Protestant translations of the Nicean Creed, this false theological emphasis on the passivity of the Virgin Mary was perpetuated by the reformers. Orthodoxy's deep awareness of the active role of the Godbirthgiver in the Incarnation was therefore lost throughout the West, to Protestants no less than to Catholics. Be that as it may, the Holy Fathers of the First Ecumenical Council explicitly state that her human role was not a passive one, but an active one, equal to the divine role of the Holy Spirit.

In assigning this equal role to the Theotokos the original Greek text implicitly recognized the importance of *"synergy,"* an aspect of the spiritual life deeply rooted in Orthodox consciousness. By *"synergy"* is meant the working together of man with God to attain salvation. It is moreover an emphasis that often seems forgotten by western Christians, given their preoccupations with philosophical concepts by which they attempt to explain the inexplicable and define the undefinable. By recognizing that the Incarnation was the fruit of the synergy resulting from the holy Virgin's working as an equal agent with the Holy Spirit, Orthodoxy still maintains that synergy is the divinely appointed way for Christ to continue to be brought forth in the world, that the glory of the Father may be seen and God glorified.

Emphasis on synergy protects Orthodoxy from pitting the human against the divine or the divine against the human. The tragic schism led by Martin Luther within western Christendom in the early XVI. century, can be directly tied to his basic misunderstanding of synergy and how it alone made the Incarnation possible. By thinking of human faith as something separable from human works, and human works separable from faith, Luther wrought much havoc and caused many bitter misunderstandings and splits within Western Christianity.

Contrary to Luther, Orthodoxy never views faith as something static that could be seized as a human concept and opposed to works. Rather is faith a living, dynamic expression of the energies of God at work within the believer through the Holy Spirit. Such a living faith by its very existence influences one's life and, just by being itself, bears fruit through its works. *"Faith, if it hath not works, is dead"* (Jas 2:17), we are taught by St. James.

In Orthodoxy neither "faith" nor "works" is conceivable apart from the Spirit at work in man, mutually animating both faith and works by the divine energies. Man's human energies reply to the divine ones and work with them, just as happened in the Incarnation of God in Jesus Christ *"by the Holy Spirit and the Virgin Mary,"* as the holy fathers of the First Ecumenical Council so succinctly put it in 325.

Does experience not prove, again and again, that if the action of God in us is to become efficacious, it must be met with a favorable response from within ourselves? In the first century either Saul of Tarsus or Ananias might have refused the meeting in the Damascus street called "Straight" (Acts 9:11), thereby evading the designs of God. But that the glory of the God of Israel might be manifest to the non-Jews, bringing them into the Kingdom of the Holy Trinity through St. Paul, both Saul and Ananias freely cooperated with the promptings of the Spirit. Saul thereby became Paul. He confessed the Lord Jesus and was baptized by Ananias who, so shortly before, had feared him as his mortal enemy.

iii

The Godbirthgiver, in a deep mystical sense, does indeed contain within herself the *whole* of the mystery of the Church. This is true in that the continuation of the Incarnation of Christ carried out by the Church was in fact already contained within what T. S. Eliot termed her *"barely prayable prayer of the one Annunciation,"* that is: *"Behold the handmaid of the*

135

MYSTERY OF THE CHURCH

Lord: be it unto me according to thy word" (Lk 1:38). Her womb thus became a throne for the King of all and, as we sing in St. Basil's liturgy, her abdominal cavity, *"wider than the heavens."* Indeed, the Creator of heaven and earth was historically contained within the belly of the Most Holy Godbirthgiver. By her, as the *Akathist Hymn* states, the Creator became a babe and had Himself carried, confounding not only men, but angels.

The Theotokos' action of bringing forth Christ in the flesh from out of her own body serves as a prototype, mystically revealing not only the mission of every Christian soul, but also the mission of the Church as the Bride of Christ. Just as the holy Godbirthgiver brought Him forth, so, ever since, has the Church continued to bring Him forth in the flesh of her faithful whereby, within the mystery of the Church, and through the Holy Spirit, He is still at work in the world.

Regardless of the century or the geographic location in which the Orthodox Church is found, her only reason for existing is always that of showing Him forth, of making Him manifest in this world. Being rooted in the kingdom of the Father, Son and Holy Spirit alone, and never really at home in an earthly kingdom, Orthodoxy, in its fidelity to the fullness of apostolic tradition, is easily distinguishable from the heterodoxy of Catholicism and Protestantism. Like the holy Apostles, the Orthodox Church is in this world, but not of it.

How otherwise could those motley men of Galilee, who gapingly stood *"gazing up into heaven"* (Acts 1:11) after the ascended Lord, have scattered after Pentecost to proclaim the truth of His Resurrection, thereby preparing for the conversion of that very Empire whose soldiers slew the Lord of Glory? Rooted in His kingdom, which *"is not of this world"* (Jn 18:36), they showed Him forth through their preaching of His Resurrection, offering an answer to the fallen race's incurable flaw: mortality. To bring Him forth and announce His kingdom, they left family and security behind, unflinchingly facing persecution, torture and, in most cases, violent martyrdom, whether by the sword, crucifixion, stoning or hideously being flayed alive.

The extent to which either the individual or the Church in a given place "brings forth Christ" in communion with the Godbirthgiver is the extent to which that individual, or the Church in that place, fulfills the vocation assigned the human race within the divine economy by God Himself. This has indeed been demonstrated by the Theotokos. Through the first Eve, Adam fell from his vocation of showing forth the glory of the Father, but in God's great mercy, man has been restored to the possibility of realizing this same vocation through the new Eve, Mary.

This vocation is moreover inseparable from the vocation of Christ our God Himself who came to show forth the glory He had with the Father before the world began. That glory, first revealed in its fullness as Trinity at the Baptism of the Son, has continued over the centuries to be seen within holy Orthodoxy. Through the mystery of the Church it is renewed both separately in individuals, and collectively in the Church through the Holy Spirit. Both bring forth Christ whose glory with the Father can be seen, for both individuals and the Church are called to become visible "Godbearers" as was St. Ignatius of Antioch.

MYSTERY OF THE CHURCH

iv

Just as the Old Testament covenant with God was realized through circumcision, animal sacrifice and the fulfillment of scores of rites of purification, so also is the New Testament covenant with God, within the mystery of the Church, also still visible in the world. It is also still tangible because it involves the transfiguration of human flesh and blood through the Sacraments.

Orthodoxy's steadfast devotion to relics is a manifestation of this visible and tangible dimension of the New Covenant of God with man through Christ. Martyr's bodies, charged by the energies of God when alive to show forth God, sometimes, after death, still gloriously manifest extraordinary powers. St. Augustine of Hippo, the Latin Father for whom the relic-hating reformers had the highest esteem, accepted as quite natural that the discovery of martyrs' relics would produce miracles. This, however, was a dimension his intellectually oriented, reformer-disciples were not about to embrace, being, as they were, proud, educated children of the Renaissance.

The visible and tangible witness of wonder-working relics therefore did not originate in the Orthodox Church of the last thousand years, nor is it peculiar to her. Relics are a basic part of the Holy Tradition of apostolic Christianity as it was understood and practiced for the first thousand years of Christian history by the undivided Church. This is something we have already found movingly in evidence following the martyrdom of St. Ignatius of Antioch, commemorated on December 20. The arrival of his holy relics back in Antioch from Rome is still piously commemorated on the Orthodox calendar on January 29.

Many post-Vatican II Catholics today find relics embarrassing, however, and have tended to relegate them to museums as irrelevant, pious curiosities of the past, completely contrary to their place in Holy Tradition where they have ever been living vehicles of grace for the faithful. The "right glory" of the plenitude of Christ, manifest throughout Christian history through relics, has thus, in many places, become a dead issue among many Roman Catholics.

Still clinging to apostolic Christianity with its miracles and relics, Orthodoxy also betrays in her worship a certain aspiration towards a truly cosmic transfiguration in Christ of the whole of fallen creation through the great mercy of God. St. John Chrysostom in his Easter sermon proclaims:

Let all then enter into the joy of our Lord. Ye first and last receiving alike your reward; ye rich and poor, rejoice together. Ye sober and ye slothful, celebrate the day. Ye that have kept the fast and ye that have not, rejoice today; for the Table is richly laden. Fare ye royally on it. The calf is a fatted one. Let no one go away hungry. Partake ye all of the cup of faith. Enjoy ye all the riches of his goodness. Let no one grieve at his poverty; for the universal kingdom has been revealed.

Every creature, all matter, everything around one awaits the consecration of the Holy Trinity that Christ may shine forth.

Envisaging Christ as completely and totally surrounding one's existence was deeply experienced by the God-bearing

MYSTERY OF THE CHURCH

Celtic Church, responsible for converting so much of Europe to a very Orthodox Christianity prior to being arrogantly stifled by Rome's mission to Britain. In a rare surviving text written by the great St. Patrick himself we read:

> *Christ be with me, Christ within me*
> *Christ behind me, Christ before me,*
> *Christ beside me, Christ to win me,*
> *Christ to comfort and restore me,*
> *Christ beneath me, Christ above me,*
> *Christ in quiet, Christ in danger,*
> *Christ in hearts of all that love me,*
> *Christ in mouth of friend and stranger.*

Seeking Christ "*in mouth of friend and stranger*" in every encounter with one's fellow man is indeed a manifestation of the "right glory" of Holy Tradition. This is made abundantly clear in a story told of a certain desert hermit in Egypt.

After many years of rigorous asceticism and what he himself esteemed to be considerable "progress" in his striving, this particular hermit one day asked God: "*Where is there anyone more advanced than I am?*" In answer he was directed to leave the desert and go into the city to a certain cobbler's shop. He hastened into the city and found the shop with the cobbler seated outside it, at work at his last. Was it really possible that it was this that he had been divinely ordered to come into the city to see? Only gradually did the proud hermit become aware of the fact that the cobbler was, in fact, actually reacting to everyone who came past him as he worked. For every soul that passed he unfailingly uttered the phrase, "*Glory to God!*" There were no exceptions: male and female, young and old, rich and poor, well-dressed and badly dressed, each one equally evoked the cobbler's praise: *"Glory to God!"*

So it was that the proud hermit was divinely taught by the humble cobbler. By merely recognizing the divine image of God in all those God directed to pass by his shop, the cobbler had shown himself more "advanced" in the spiritual way than the hermit, surpassing all the "progress" the hermit proudly thought he had made during his years of asceticism. Forgetting self, the cobbler had become a vase for the glory of God to enter the world, a veritable conduit to lost paradise.

One may say that the Godbirthgiver, in becoming a unique gage offered by men to God has revealed the cosmic potential for all flesh. She went beyond Abraham's covenant of the Old Testament. Abraham's covenant was strictly for the Jews, the chosen people, through whom was provided the indispensable framework out of which the Theotokos was to be born. Her own covenant, however, that of the New Testament, was for the salvation of the entire human race, and thus far greater than Abraham's precursory one of the Old Testament. When the Fruit of the womb of the Virgin Mary descended to Hades to announce His victory over Death to Adam and all his descendants, He thereby indeed became *"the glory of thy people, Israel" (Lk 2:32)*, gloriously fulfilling also the prophecy of Isaiah (Isa 49:6) and of the ancient Simeon by becoming a *"Light to lighten the Gentiles"* (Lk 2:32). Indeed in Him was to be found the veritable emptying out of the glory of the Father, full of grace and truth, to the extent that mortal man could bear to look upon Him.

The canticle of the Theotokos, *"My soul doth magnify the Lord" (Lk 1:46)*, provides the basis for the last of the nine odes of Orthodoxy's "Canon." The Canon is a set of texts commemorating various instances of God's intervention to bring salvation in the Old Testament. Notable examples are the saving of Moses and the Hebrews from Pharaoh at the waters of the Red Sea, of Jonah from the belly of the great fish, and of the wondrous deliverance of the three Hebrew youths from the fiery furnace of Babylon. But the supreme instance, indeed, the crowning instance of God's salvation of the race, was the Incarnation, announced by the Virgin's canticle celebrating her being chosen to conceive the Savior.

It is for this reason that at Matins, just before the ninth ode begins, the priest, smoking censer in hand, emerges from the altar and, turning towards the icon of the Theotokos on the left of the Holy Doors, admonishes the faithful: "*Let us extol in song the Godbirthgiver and Mother of the Light.*" A complete censing of the entire church and congregation follows while the choir sings the holy Virgin's canticle, known in the West as the "Magnificat" (Lk 1:46-55). The verses of the "Magnificat" are moreover sandwiched between the lines of the very Orthodox hymn of magnification for the Theotokos:

> *Higher art thou than the Cherubim!*
> *And beyond compare more glorious than the Seraphim!*
> *Thou who without stain bearest God the Word,*
> *Thee, truly Theotokos, do we magnify*!

As always in Orthodoxy, far more than a mere ritualistic action is involved. During that solemn censing of the whole church and congregation, every believer is being reminded

142

that it was a female human agent through whom the saving Light came, He who was *"the way, the truth and the life"* (Jn 14:6). Every believer is thus being subtly challenged to recall the potential of his own humanity to bring forth Christ, taking as a role-model this member of the human race who, by working with the Holy Spirit, made God manifest to her race to save that race from death.

Orthodox Christians rejoice, week after week, at God's appearing to them in the flesh, repeatedly singing as Matins begins: *"God is the Lord and hath appeared unto us!"* So also does the rejoicing in the ninth ode confirm for the Orthodox that the Incarnation through the most holy Godbirthgiver and Ever-Virgin Mary by no means ended with the Ascension of Christ. His incarnation continues quietly in all those baptized in His name, as well as gloriously and visibly manifest in the flesh and blood offered by the martyrs, saints and confessors who continue to perpetuate His incarnate presence within the mystery of the Church. All of this is inseparable from the Theotokos, as also from her role in the divine economy.

Because of the centrality of the role of the Theotokos in Orthodox thought, worship and life, Orthodox Christians find it impossible to conceive of trying to measure or discuss their devotion to her, much less to entertain it as a subject for debate. A common ground seemingly shared by Catholicism and Protestantism, and one invariably noted by the Orthodox, is that of their ever-evolving, ever-shifting attitudes concerning "devotion" given the Godbirthgiver. Protestant rejection of her cult in the XVI. century was indeed but a manifestation of tendencies already latent in Roman Catholicism. Today that Protestant tendency is not hard to discern in many modern Roman Catholics who manifest considerable ambiguity in regard to the Godbirthgiver. This is something impossible for Orthodox Christians to comprehend outside a purely Protestant context.

The Vatican's action in 1950 of defining exactly just how the Assumption of the Godbirthgiver took place, declaring belief in Rome's man-made definition a dogma essential to salvation, could only strike the Orthodox as sadly misplaced emphasis. Orthodoxy has never felt any need to make official proclamations about how the most holy Godbirthgiver was taken from earth to heaven since all Orthodox believe it through that Holy Tradition that is such a living part of the life of her faithful. In honor of August 15 a two-week Lenten fast is kept from August first through the fourteenth, plus frequent--often daily--fervent singings of the Little Supplicatory Canon (*Paraclesis*) to her during this time.

As with so much involving the cult of the Godbirthgiver in Orthodoxy, the events of August 15 are, however, treated as a sort of discreet family secret, talked about only in the family. One grasps that outsiders would not, indeed, could not begin to understand. Indeed, how can one who denies the Incarnation itself be asked to confront such a mystery? It is out of a truly familial love and tradition that the Orthodox approach this completely undefined mystery, much as they also approach the annual miracle of the Holy Fire in Jerusalem's Church of the Holy Sepulchre on Holy Saturday.

Roman Catholics of course find it hard to understand that it is in fact Orthodoxy's deep and loving intimacy with the holy Theotokos, and with the mystery of her unassailable place in Holy Tradition, that motivates Orthodoxy's categorical repudiation of the Vatican's strange 1858 dogma of the Immaculate Conception. Orthodoxy realized that man-made dogma, based on rational speculation and on no revealed facts whatsoever, would, by freeing her from the sin of Adam at the moment of her conception, thereby seem to cause the Theotokos to rise above the human race. The flesh which she gave the Word for His Incarnation would therefore no longer really be a part of the flesh we share with Him, but a hyper-holy flesh. This rejection of the Roman dogma in no way, however, affects the deep Orthodox understanding that the most holy Theotokos was without sin.

Indeed, a strange irony continues to plague the dogma of the Immaculate Conception within the Roman Church where many believers confound it with the universal Christian dogma of the virgin birth of Jesus Christ. Whence the not inconsiderable scandal when such uninformed Roman Catholics discover that the Orthodox Church does not believe in their 1858 dogma of the Immaculate Conception!

Finally, the dynamics of the Orthodox believer's relationship with the Godbirthgiver plays such an integral role in his own personal experience of the mystery of the Church that he cannot conceive of the "right glory" of apostolic Christianity without that personal, very female dimension accorded by the powerful presence and protection of her unceasing and powerful intercessions. Were her prayers prior to Pentecost not treasured by the Apostles? Is her icon, with her showing forth the merciful Christ, not in truth Orthodoxy's most universally recognizable image? Is her tenderness not Orthodoxy's most universal characteristic?

The Orthodox Christian's personal life in Christ is therefore, above all else, rooted not only in his intimacy with

God, but also in his intimacy with the most holy Godbirthgiver. In this double mystery is the source sustaining his personal striving towards the Uncreated Light, the Bridegroom, Jesus Christ, *"the brightness of the holy Father's glory."*

The humble and pious Orthodox Christian therefore struggles to learn through her intercessions to pray with her before every eventuality: *"Behold the handmaid of the Lord: be it unto me according to thy word."* To the extent that he becomes united with her in this prayer, he too, through God's great mercy to him, may also become an incarnation of the mystery of the Church and, like her, also become its protector. In the light of the Holy Spirit it may even be given him at times to grasp, ever so fleetingly, the glory that is hers, that glory of being, for all eternity, a living pledge, offered by a fallen human race to its Creator, that Christ may be *"all, and in all"* (Col 3:11).

APPENDIX

Author's Note

The following article, *"Sent by God,"* was written almost a decade ago at the request of the editor of *Ephipany, A Journal of Faith and Insight* for a special number of that journal dealing with conversions to Orthodoxy (Vol II, no. 1, Fall, 1990). Its inclusion here is at the suggestion of Regina Orthodox Press.

--William Bush

SENT BY GOD...

Man begins a life-long pilgrimage the day he is born. The variety of circumstances governing and shaping that pilgrimage are seemingly infinite, so vast is the greatness of God's creation around us. The spot where man is born, the parents given him, his social condition and his background--man really has nothing to do with all those variables. All is given. And, since all is given, it is a gift to be born into a Christian home, a grace, something totally unmerited on our part.

Each of us, by the grace of God, starts where he can. Every pilgrimage has the potential of being a good one if, in the end, it leads back to Him who gave it. On my own pilgrimage, the door to Orthodoxy was to be opened for me through an encounter which I neither sought, nor could possibly ever have imagined. After 44 years it still remains as wondrously life-giving as it was the day it occurred.

Yet my beginnings were banal enough: a small farm town in central Florida boasting three large churches with steeples dominating the town's 8,000 inhabitants: the First Baptist, the First Methodist, and the First Presbyterian. A tiny Episcopal structure housed services twice a month. The neat, solid, but very small red-brick Roman Catholic parish catered largely to out-lying Hungarian farmers.

It was to the imposing First Baptist Church that my mother was attached and to which she took us three children, I being the oldest by three years. My father tagged along. Since rejection of infant baptism is one of the basic tenets of the Baptists, and since baptism is given only on demand, everything within the Baptist church seemed designed to exert pressure that such a demand be made, each service concluding with an invitation to "walk the aisle" and confess Christ and be baptized.

Beginning at the age of nine when I started "staying for church" after the hour-long Sunday School--a real high point in a drab

148

Sent by God   William Bush

week in those pre-television, depression days of the 1930s--I plunged into a miserable period of despair lasting until I was twelve. Every Saturday night as I cleaned the family shoes for Sunday church, my soul was caught in the clutches of a hideous inner crisis. I'd contemplate the fires of hell I knew I'd be assigned to should I die the following week without having "walked the aisle" the next day. Yet I was unable to muster the courage to speak of something so intimate to my mother. Thus my dialogue with God was an anguished one. I believed--how I believed!--but the social and psychological barriers requiring me to be the center of a public spectacle held me back. Finally, one Sunday morning when I was twelve years old, motivated by a visiting evangelist, I found the courage to express that desire to my mother, just before we slipped into church after Sunday School.

Baptism followed a few weeks later in the church's large baptistry on a Sunday evening. Waiting with the other candidates in a hallway while the minister was off donning the fisherman's rubber trouser-boots he always wore under his jacket for baptism, I was filled with a strong sense of awe, even as I continued to be when I entered the pool and was plunged under in the name of the Holy Trinity. Thus when the well-meaning deacon, posted in the hallway leading out of the baptistry, asked me as I emerged, dripping wet, "Was it cold?" I was dumbfounded. To me it seemed almost blasphemous in its banality. Baptized in the Name of the Father, the Son and the Holy Spirit, had I not now been joined to that countless company of Christians who, though I knew not quite how, did, historically stretch from the New Testament down to my local First Baptist Church? Completely caught up in what I believe involved the *whole* of all that I was or could ever hope to be, in this life or the next, such temporal realities as the temperature of the water in the Baptist baptistry that evening seemed in that moment totally irrelevant for me.

Sent by God   **William Bush**

There was, however, one event which enigmatically seemed to reverberate with what was going on inside me. Outside the church where we were parked, the young pastor came over to our car just as we were leaving. From the back seat where, clad in fresh clothes, I sat quietly with my brother and sister, absorbed in my own thoughts, I heard him say to my father--and not to my mother, which impressed me at the time--"I wanted to tell you that when I baptized your son I had a sense of not knowing what I was baptizing, of what it would make him..." Could he, even then, already sense that, by God's mercy, there indeed awaited for me something completely beyond his Baptist experience? Certainly he could never have dreamed of Orthodoxy! That strange statement still strikes me as singular, even as it did an Abbot of the Holy Mountain to whom I once confided it when he asked me to describe, in all its details, my Baptist baptism for him.

Thus my earthly pilgrimage became Christian in a white, Anglo-Saxon, fundamentalist Protestant framework. This framework was very shortly thereafter to prove lacking, however.

ii

As a rather precocious player of the piano by age 13, I was engaged by our next-door neighbor as "organist"--the instrument was actually a harmonium--for the twice-monthly services at the tiny Episcopal Church. This lady was one of the tiny handful of Anglicans in our town where Episcopalians were a much rarer brand of Christian even than Roman Catholics.

I, at 13, completely bereft of all knowledge even of the existence of liturgical life beyond the three celebrations punctuating the Baptist church year, that is, Christmas, Easter, and "Mother's Day," devoured the *Book of Common Prayer* and, in particular, the fine print concerning the church calender with its Easter cycle, saints days, feast and fast days. How *rich* life suddenly seemed: time could be consecrated, made *holy*, other than by Christmas or

150

the secular "Mother's Day!" As for Easter, it was unbelievable in its dimensions, being all tied up with pre-Lent and Lent as well as with Whitsunday and all that followed it. What a wonderful discovery it was!

In addition to gaining this sense of the consecration of time, I found myself also captivated by the idea that the Anglicans prayed that they might receive the Body and Blood of Jesus Christ in Holy Communion. Moreover, the tiny parish was in "high church" territory and I became familiar with certain people crossing themselves and genuflecting; with the choir, processing behind a cross and bowing before the altar. All of this spoke to me of an awareness of the sacred which actually was expressed in the here and now, something I had intuited when I saw actors cross themselves in certain films at the local "picture show."

The only glimmer of the sacred I had ever had in the Baptist Church was the feeling I got when, once every three months, I would see the "memorial table" in front of the huge central pulpit stacked high with plates of matzos and special round trays housing hundreds of thimble-sized glasses filled with grape juice for the quarterly "Lord's Supper," the whole solemnly covered with a long white cloth hanging down. Before this quarterly spectacle I had a deep sense that this was something different from *ordinary* life, something peculiarly *Christian*, something which non-Christians would *not* do. But it was my initial encounter with Orthodoxy which was finally to give me an idea of how glorious, wonderful and intense the sacred could become in this life.

iii

I had always known that Greek Orthodoxy existed. Tarpon Springs, a Greek sponge-fishing town, was nearby and the Archbishop from New York, plus thousands of other Greeks, unfailingly converged there every January 6 to celebrate the Lord's Baptism. The annual two-page spread in the Tampa paper with photographs of the bearded clergy, high school band, and dripping young diver receiving the Archbishop's blessing for having retrieved the prelate's hand-cross from the water, was always accompanied by some journalistic statement   about Greek Orthodoxy being "a very ancient form of Christianity." The summer of my fourteenth birthday I was to run head-on into this "very ancient form of Christianity."

A local Greek had died and the priest was brought from Tarpon Springs to hold the funeral in the Episcopal church. I, as the "organist," was advised by ladies of the parish to be on hand should the Greeks want any music. Needless to say, the old harmonium was silent that afternoon once the service got started. Not only was everything sung, but the cantor's style seemed to me positively goat-like--more a bleating than singing. The great procession into the church with the coffin born on the shoulders of the pallbearers, the Baptist widow and half-Greek children and all the Greeks following as the priest, swinging censer and answered by the bleating of the cantor: all of that was so totally out of character with the calm dignity I had come to love and respect in the tiny Episcopal parish that, even though my own sentiments were quite other than hers, I did understand our neighbor's saying the next day, "I thought I was in the jungles of darkest Africa!"

Like a seismograph, the face of our town's portly Baptist undertaker registered highs and lows of shock as the service proceeded. Advised by the parish ladies that the coffin was *never* opened in the Episcopal church, he was initially disconcerted when ordered by the priest's translator to open up the coffin before beginning the service. After the unprecedented rite of the "last kiss" at the end of the service, he also had to stand helplessly by, wide-eyed and sweating behind his glasses as he and I (pinned behind the harmonium and unable to budge as my escape route was blocked by the open coffin) watched the priest cover the face and shoulders of the deceased with a tube-shaped sheaf of material reassembling white satin. But that was mild compared with the record shock registered on his face at the grave when the translator ordered the coffin opened yet again and the priest anointed the white cloth with oil and wine and a scoop of earth...

These exterior things were of little value for me in the end, however. What I think I really took with me from that service was my memory of seeing the wives of the local restaurant and liquor store owners--social pariah to Baptists--crossing themselves *in response* to what was being chanted by the priest and his unforgettable cantor. Though I felt terribly out of place in my cassock and surplice in the front of the church at the harmonium, I realized that I was totally unimportant for these Greeks who had no more eyes for me than for a fly on the wall. They were actively *participating* in a dimension which had suddenly been made accessible to them, and that dimension, I sensed, had nothing at all to do with our neighbor's "darkest Africa." In a strange way I could not quite grasp, I did feel however it had a great deal to do with Jesus Christ, with Him whose crucified image had ever burned in the depths of my heart. For, even as a very small Baptist child, I had instinctively understood that the sufferings of God were, by some inexplicable mystery, for *me*, as for *all* men. Of course, such thoughts would probably have been considered "exaggerated" and "excessive," had I tried to express them and I would have been said to have taken things much "too seriously" and to be really just "too sensitive."

Yet that afternoon I think I did make a tentative connection between my deep, instinctive feelings and the quite extraordinary things going on around me. The priest with his hand-cross and his grating cantor, the clouds of incense: all this somehow *allowed* these normally uninteresting people to spring into life before my eyes, to be connected to a world which not only was obviously dearer and more real to them than anything existing in our small Florida town, but was also a world where He whom I loved was

Lord and God. But how might I ever begin to hope to gain access
to that wonderful, unexplored world where I sensed I would find
Jesus Christ in a new fullness, where I felt He must be *as He is* and
not as men *said* He was?

iv

Certainly the local tiny Roman Catholic parish fascinated me.
I would peer inside at the statues and candles through the tiny
church's glass-paneled doors when no one was on the street to see
me. I read avidly in the local weekly about the Good Friday
services and the veneration before the manger at Christmas.

Thus the Christmas of my fourteenth year I obtained my
mother's permission to attend the Midnight Mass, accompanied by
my great boyhood Baptist friend who was also interested in
religion. From this encounter, about which my friend and I must
have talked non-stop during the week following, came about our
custom, Baptists though we were, of visiting Roman Catholic
churches whenever we went to nearby Tampa. The colorful Jesuit
church of the Sacred Heart was our favorite. We had learned to
cross ourselves, to genuflect and, for all external appearances, to
behave as "Catholics." For my own part this was not from any
intention to appear something I was not, but rather from an
instinctive need to enter into communion with those others who
were praying there, whether lighting candles, making the Stations
of the Cross, or telling their beads. Somehow what they were
doing, even though not fully grasped, did seem extremely *relevant*
to me and drew me like a magnet: they, like me, sensed a *need* to
express love for Jesus Christ.

By God's grace my familiarity with Anglican worship and an
organ scholarship at a nearby university placed me during my
university years as organist and choirmaster in a sizeable
Episcopal parish with an excellent priest to whom my debt is
enormous. He grounded me in theology and gave me a grasp of
what had happened historically between the New Testament and

the present. In particular, he insisted on the triumph of the true Christian faith over all the great heresies.

Yet I had difficulty in entering the Anglican church because of infant baptism. I failed to see the logic of saying sponsors could suffice for receiving Baptism, but not for the reception of Confirmation and Holy Communion afterward. Finally my good priest said, "Well, there is a Church you'd find logical. It's the Orthodox Church. That's the way they do it. All is given the baby immediately after baptism."

Strangely enough this consoled me. I became Anglican, and as such, continued my Christian pilgrimage for the next 18 years, frequenting Anglican monasteries, shrines and high church parishes on both sides of the Atlantic, and teaching in Anglican institutions. Yet I had learned the Jesus Prayer from my university priest as well as a real veneration for the Orthodox. He, after all, would always refer to the Greeks as being in the "true Church" whenever they came from time to time for a funeral or an occasional Divine Liturgy which I would try to attend.

Work in an Episcopal Indian mission school in South Dakota, a Master's degree in French literature with a thesis on the great French Christian writer, Georges Bernanos (to whom I have since devoted my career as a scholar), a summer studying in France in 1953, and, finally, a year in Haiti teaching English at the tiny Anglican seminary, all these were necessary for me to come, finally, to believe in the power of the Enemy. I had not yet grasped, in spite of Bernanos' *Under the Sun of Satan*, that one can *will* participation with the powers of darkness. Until my experience in Haiti I had rather a rose-colored view of evil, not understanding that when one encounters it, the side one wants to be on must be *consciously* chosen.

I emerged from my experiences there not only understanding that one sign of the cross is more powerful than all the powers of darkness, but also that those powers of darkness are *always* there within us, every bit as much as without, and ever ready to attack.

Orthodoxy, with what I sensed must be its powerful "very ancient" defenses against the demonic, often flashed in my thoughts when reflected upon the dark forces I'd confronted in Haiti. Then, just prior to my 26th birthday, I was to experience an encounter unique in my life.

v

My interest in Bernanos had brought me back to France a second time, though most of that summer was to be spent in Austria to improve my German. I had but a week in Paris with one single Sunday: June 24, 1955, the feast of the Birth of the Forerunner, John the Baptist. My boyhood ex-Baptist friend, the same with whom I had gone to my first Mass, was then finishing a year's study there before entering a Roman Catholic seminary. Among the possibilities for Sunday he suggested the Russian cathedral on the rue Daru to hear the magnificent bass voice of the Deacon.

So it was that I found myself plunged into a world which seemed to me to resemble heaven itself. I was immediately happy and completely at peace within. Yet I was so filled with infinite, longing love for *Him* whose presence I so strongly sensed in that place that tears streamed down my face. I think even I must have suffered from some sort of psychic paralysis for when I reached the middle of the church, that is where I remained, as if transfixed, while my friend withdrew to the side to prop up.

Everything spoke to me: the light coming through the windowed dome above played on the clouds of incense in which the faithful silently moved about lighting whole seas of candles or making prostrations; the rise and fall of the swelling Russian chants; the blessings given with the two- and three-branched candelabra by the venerable Metropolitan Vladimir, his eyes raised to heaven. One sensed that he was fully aware that through his action divine protection was being called down on us standing before him.

156

Sent by God   William Bush

I, American ex-Southern Baptist turned Anglo-Catholic, felt I
had died and gone to heaven. I *tried* to participate, crossing
myself when most of the people seemed to do so, and kneeling
when most of them did. And even though I was not quite sure
why, I was sure that it was all good, very, very *good*, and that for
the first time in my life I was doing what I had been created for:
standing before God with all those others who also believed and,
like me, were *happy* to stand before Him in love, even as tears also
flooded their faces.

On my immediate left stood a thin, severe, fiftyish female figure
in a tan suede jacket. She wore pearls in her ears and her hair was
pulled tightly back in a bun, but I did not study her face. Yet I
could not be indifferent to her presence there, standing quietly,
stiffly, severely even, for more than two hours beside me, more
reticent it seemed to me with her thoughtful signs of the cross than
the others.

After about an hour when my friend came over to ask if I'd had
enough and were ready to leave I declined. I had no desire to tear
myself away from those rare and unimagined riches. It was thus
an hour or so later and after the end of the service, that we moved
out into the vestibule where I stopped briefly at the tables where
icons and books were displayed to purchase a copy of the Liturgy
of Saint John Chrysostom in English. I had no sooner paid the
veiled lady standing behind the tables than I heard a voice directly
behind me. It was that of a woman, speaking English, very
authoritatively, and rolling her "r's" from her heavy Russian
accent.

"Are you English or American?" the voice asked. I turned to see
who was addressing me in such a tone in my native language in the
Russian cathedral in Paris. The lady who had stood beside me in
church was now looking at me out of pale blue eyes such as I had
never known before nor ever seen since. She did not smile. She
showed no warmth, none of that friendliness North Americans

expect. There was nothing but that intense, penetrating, unforgettable look as she awaited my answer to her banal question.

"I'm American," I answered, "I'm Anglo-Catholic."

Apparently this latter bit of information did not interest her. She still neither smiled, nor showed any warmth whatsoever. There was only her stare and her unforgettable eyes.

"Have you ever seen Russian baptism?" she asked in the tone of a policewoman asking for a passport.

"Ah....uh, no!" I replied, swallowing hard, not quite knowing what was expected of me in such a circumstance, as the Russian faithful pushed past us.

When I think of it now, I think that as we stood there, silently facing one another in tense confrontation in the vestibule, we must somehow both have been aware that we had not really ceased standing expectantly before God and His great mystery, just as we had been doing for over two hours.

She spoke again, her eyes still fixed on me.

"I have home for children. Chateau. Outside Paris. This afternoon we baptize five children. Big children. You come!"

How could I not be intrigued by such an invitation? But I was with my friend.

"That would be very interesting," I replied, not wanting to sound impolite, "but I'm with a friend."

"No place in my car for friend. One place! You come."

Facing her unsmiling stare, I realized that she was determined that her invitation not be politely dismissed without a serious effort on my part to accept it. I excused myself, spoke with my friend who, as a Catholic convert, had no interest whatsoever in seeing "Russian baptism." I thus returned to her, standing there in the doorway, and said, "Yes, thank you, I should be pleased to go".

I was to meet her back in front of the church at one o'clock. My friend and I thus had a quick lunch nearby before I left him to go back to the church to meet this mysterious new acquaintance.

vi

She drove up in front of the church behind the steering wheel of the most humble of French cars: a *Deux-chevaux*, its body made of corrugated tin, its windows and windshield a combination of push-outs and prop-ups. She got out, we shook hands, as one does in France, then she explained that when she picked up the two Godparents the old Russian-speaking lady would sit in front beside her while the Cypriot seminarian, who spoke English, would sit in back with me. But, for the moment, I might sit in front. I got in as did she. Before starting her little car however, she stared through the prop-up windshield, and spoke softly to no one in particular. Obviously she was weighing many things. She seemed to be concentrating very deeply with all her being.

"My people would condemn me for speaking in this way to a total stranger," she said in a demi-whisper defying any comment on my part. "But who knows? Sometimes things happen..."

She started the car and, suddenly, totally in contrast with her great reserve up until that moment, cheerfully asked with the brightest possible optimism and her first smile, "Do you know my brother?"

This adventure was getting beyond me. I did not even know this stranger's name and here she was asking me if I knew her brother!

Rather lamely I asked, "Uh... who uh... who is your brother?"

With the great dignity she always displayed when speaking of her Oxford professor older brother, she drew up her shoulders, even as she drove, and very proudly pronounced the five syllables of "Ni-cho-las Zer-nov," finishing with a flourish.

"Oh yes!" I said with considerable relief, "He writes books on the Russian Church."

The conversation became easier. She so desperately wanted me to read his book, *The Reintegration of the Church* that she made, if I recall correctly, a sudden U-turn in a Paris street to detour back by her apartment at 395 rue de Vaugirard--the future scene of some of the most vivid and decisive hours of my life--to seek this book. She brought it down to me in the car before going on to collect the two Godparents. I was to read the book, she instructed me, and return it to her when I came back through Paris from Austria that summer on my way home to Wisconsin.

vii

My arrival that afternoon at the Moulin de Senlis at Montgeron was to be as magic and full of wonder as had been all leading up to it. Originally a hunting lodge for Henry IV, its ivy-covered turrets and mill-wheel, its large courtyard surrounded by outbuildings set on the edge of an ivy-carpeted wood along the Yerre in the lush heart of the Ile de France--all of that was of an indescribable charm and beauty and so unlike North America. For me that day I found it so completely worthy of the mysterious Sophia Zernoff who had brought me there without my even being too sure of her name.

Prior to the baptism I, with other visitors, was taken by her on a tour of the "chateau." When I saw names such "Rachmaninoff" and "Kandinsky" posted on various dormitories signifying these great Russian artists' contribution to this children's home I realized that my new friend must move in very high circles. I was still ignorant of the fact that Sophia Miahilovna Zernova was probably the best-known Russian woman in Paris, admired for selflessly devoting her adult life to aiding eastern European refugees find housing and jobs in the French capital. Her children's home had grown out of the need for these refugees' children to be looked after and sent to school while their parents worked. For years the great adventure in faith lived by "Sophia Miahilovna," as she was respectfully known to every Russian in Paris, inspired those who met her. The French government too showed its esteem when, after, 40 years, she finally applied for a French passport. All normal fees were waived and the passport presented with ceremony, saying they wanted "Mademoiselle Zernoff" to know by that gesture how much the French government *wanted* her to be French.

Two things in particular remain with me from that afternoon, quite apart from the baptism, which was a whole world in itself, even as the morning liturgy at the cathedral had been. The first has to do with one of those *"very strange happenings,"* to quote Dr. Nicholas Zernov, speaking to me once in Oxford after Sophia Miahilovna's death regarding the many miracles in her life. The second thing concerned her deep and penetrating understanding of the truth about man and God.

Our little group of some twenty had completed the tour of the buildings and were standing in a circle in the middle of the central courtyard. Sophia Mihailovna was just opposite me on the other side of the largish circle. She looked over at me, the only non-Orthodox, and said rather pointedly as she fixed me with her blue eyes: "I can tell this since we are all *believers,"* insisting on that last word as she stared at me.

She then told how, after all her contributions were in, not only from the Rachmaninoffs and Kandinskys, but also from the French government and all church organizations, she had received one morning at her refugee office the bill for converting the chateau's barn into the boy's dormitory. She had nothing with which to pay it. Nor did she have any further sources to tap for that urgently needed sum.

"I remembered then, as I wondered what I was going to do, that *He* said that if we ask for something in *His* name that *He* will give it us. And do you know why this is so?" she asked, once more looking across the circle as if to address me in particular. "It is because when we pray in *His* name it is no longer *we* who pray; it is *He* who prays in us. And that puts *fire* into our prayer so that it rises to God and is heard. So I decided to go to the church and pray in *His* name."

"Before His icon I told Him that I had come to pray in *His* name because He had promised that if we pray that way He will give us what we ask. I told Him that I had received this bill and that I had no funds to pay it. Moreover, all those children I had done this for were not *my* children, after all, but *His.* I told Him that I had done all I could. Now *He* must do something."

Sophia Mihailovna then told how, having prayed so boldly in His name, she returned to her refugee office. The morning post had arrived. In it was a letter from a Dutch student organization saying they had heard of her work in Paris and wished to make a contribution. Enclosed was a check for the exact amount of the bill, down to the last old franc, then worth less than a cent. "Had it been for *one* franc more, or *one* franc less than the bill I should have said, 'Coincidence!' But no!" she exclaimed, her eyes alight with joyous, child-like wonder, "It was the *exact* amount!"

I joined the believers in crossing myself, just as, subsequently, I would do so many, many times as my life continued to be touched by the "*very strange happenings*" taking place around this servant of God.

The second incident that afternoon allowed me to see yet another aspect of my new friend. A very little girl came running up to her in the courtyard crying. Sophia Mihailovna took her in her arms and held her, caressing her and asking her what was the matter. Another little girl, she said, had hit her and she'd done absolutely nothing to her. Still caressing her and holding her Sophia Mihailovna said very softly, staring off into the distance as she had that afternoon when I'd first got into her car, "That doesn't matter... That doesn't matter... Men are wicked. That's why we have to believe in God."

I was shattered. It was such a naked encounter with truth--a truth I can't imagine anyone else I've ever known putting quite that way. Instinctively I knew it was *true.* Yet prior to that moment I would have had difficulty in even conceiving it, much less in articulating it. Now I would never forget that statement, "That's why we *have* to believe in God." Nor would I ever forget her who had been led to make it at a cost which, even to this day, I still feel I'm only beginning to fathom.

As for the baptism itself, the warmth and joy I found all around me overwhelmed me. These people were *happy*. They were, moreover, totally, completely *relaxed* in spite of all the "formality" of the ceremony which, in Anglican circles, would have been termed "very high!" The love and affection expressed by the Godparents for the children, the way they changed their clothes down to the last stitch wrapped in a blanket in the midst of the church, and the unforgettably joyous procession around the wash-tub baptistry, carrying candles and singing *"As many of you as were baptized into Christ have put on Christ. Alleluia."*--all of that made me think that this was the way Christians were *supposed* to behave amongst themselves.

There was also, on the part of my new friend, yet another moment I shall never forget. She too was a Godparent for one of the children. When the moment came for her to "breath and spit" on that Enemy whom she had, on behalf of the child, just renounced in favor of Christ, I shall never forget the infinite, deep sadness on her face, a sadness expressing infinite regret that it had to be so in this life. I sensed her deep, sorrowing recognition that the Enemy is always there, twisting everything, and having to be renounced and fought every day, even until one's last breath.

The warmth and joy of the baptism spilled over with sit-down refreshments in the refectory where I found myself treated like a friend by everyone, stranger that I was. When I said I must leave to get back to Paris, my new friend insisted on driving me in her little car back to the Montgeron station, renewing her admonitions to read her brother's book and return it to her when I came back through Paris at the end of August.

I recall to this day those moments on the station platform, standing and waiting for the direct train back into Paris. Profoundly, acutely, almost painfully aware that nothing in my life could ever be quite the same again, I also realized that I had never before met anyone who, with so little said, had entered so deeply into that secret interior life where is fought man's lonely battle for God.

That encounter of June 24, 1955 which was to govern my spiritual destiny, also mysteriously served as a prelude to two further extraordinary encounters in the immediately ensuing days, encounters which would govern my professional destiny. I met one of Bernanos' sons and, through him, Bernanos' literary executor, the great Swiss critic, Albert Béguin, thanks to whom I was granted the following year a Fulbright Award to go to Paris where for three years I pursued my doctoral thesis at the Sorbonne.

viii

When I came back through Paris at the end of August I missed Sophia Mihailovna and left the book with the concierge. I wrote to her from Wisconsin to express my regret at not having seen her again. A short answer came around Christmas time in which she made a statement that seemed to me as extraordinary as everything else always was about her. *"I hope that some day you will come to know the fullness of Orthodoxy."*

It was the very first time in my life that I had ever conceived of it even being possible that one might *become* Orthodox without actually being *born* into it. That was such a *tremendous* concept for me. It was one which, from that point on, would obsess me. But how could such a thing be possible, except by God, with whom all things are possible?

My three years as a doctoral student at the Sorbonne made it possible for Sophia Mihailovna to open many doors for me. Not only her Oxford brother, but also Vladimir Lossky and his family, Paul Evdokimov, the young John Meyendorff--not yet a priest-- and Fr. Alexander Schmemmen all became realities to me because of her. Yet none could match the light and joy of our rather rare exchanges. To see her eyes burn with the light of God whenever she pronounced, "Jesus Christ," or joyously said, with all her being, "Christ is risen!" was an unforgettable experience.

Thanks to her I also met at Paris' St. Sergius Seminary two students fresh from the States who introduced me to all sorts of Orthodox milieux I'd never have penetrated otherwise. Thus came about a seemingly miraculous encounter with an elderly Russian nun, a princess of the old regime, speaking to me in impeccably aristocratic English.

Staring at me without having proffered the slightest word of greeting, her very first words were a question: "Are you Orthodox?"

"No, but I am interested in Orthodoxy."

"If you are interested in Orthodoxy there is a book you must read. I'm an old woman and crippled, but I'm going upstairs to get it to show you so that you may get it."

Thus, by this miraculously instantaneous exchange I discovered the *Philokalia* and the prayer of the heart. It was God's gentle, merciful answer to my six-year search for spiritual reading which would take me beyond the limits of *The Imitation of Christ*, introduced to me by my Anglican priest and read repeatedly.

Still, I yet had to see my first Orthodox Easter. Thanks to my American seminarian friends the services of Great and Holy Week at the seminary in 1957 acclimatized me for the annual miracle that every Orthodox Easter is. On the Friday following Easter-- Feast of the Theotokos as the Life-Giving Fountain--Sophia Miahilovna invited me to supper. I was happy to be able to speak with someone about all I felt within me after Orthodox Easter, having at last discovered *"my own kind"* of Christians: people who not only *said* they believed He really had come out of the tomb, but who actually *shouted*, "Christ is risen!" leaving no doubt that it was the most important thing in their life. I could not stop talking about all this.

Sophia Mihailovna, in the maid's apartment she occupied up beyond where the elevator stopped in the building housing her second brother's doctor's office, had gone into her little kitchen for something. I heard her calling back, "Yes! Now you want to be Orthodox!"

I had not yet faced the issue squarely. The impossibility of it all haunted me if I allowed myself to think about it. There were so many off-putting complications which would inevitably be added to one's life, whether linguistic, ethnic or other. I swallowed hard, my heart pounding, and finally stammered a rather uncomfortable "...Yes!"

Sophia Mihailovna's answer shot back from her tiny kitchen with no delay: "Wait ten years..."

God had spoken. We talked of other things.

For the next ten years I thus explored and *loved* Orthodoxy with none of those wearisome practical parish obligations such as have become my lot now at the end of my life, sometimes joyful, sometimes painful, always pressing, even as Sophia Mihailovna's refugees' needs must always have been pressing for her until she was forced to her bed by her long, last illness. During those ten years I married in England an Anglican vicar's daughter whom I had also met in Paris. By God's mercy we baptized our four children in the Anglican Church.

The end of those ten years coincided with our family move from Duke University in North Carolina, after seven years, to the University of Western Ontario in London, Canada. And, as everything is given, I realized that it was neither by "chance" nor by "coincidence" that in London, Ontario, Sophia Mihailovna had "a great friend who thinks like me on everything."

Slightly younger than Sophia Mihailovna, this great Russian lady, daughter of the last tsarist admiral of the Baltic fleet and descended from a converted Tartar prince, had carried her youngest child 3,000 miles in her arms during the Stalinist persecutions to a supposedly bed-ridden surviving priest to get him secretly baptized. She proved of such great help as I moved towards the end of my long pilgrimage to Orthodoxy. Thus, by

Sent by God   William Bush

God's grace and help, I entered into "the fullness of Orthodoxy" by chrismation in the Greek Church on March 25, 1967, feast of the Annunciation to the Most Holy Godbirthgiver, ending more than a quarter century of soul-searching since my Baptist baptism the summer of 1941.

It was neither an easy nor a painless completion. On one hand I was completely crushed and devastated by the solitary impossibility of what I was doing. For, if for me personally it was the completion and fulfillment of all my soul's deepest longings, on a practical, intimate level it represented a break with so much which even many Orthodox regarded as peculiar. Still, I knew I had to choose Orthodoxy if I were to remain Christian, and being a Christian, I knew, was the only unperishable thing that we are ever given in this life. Like those who took the path towards Christ in the early days when such a path could only lead to martyrdom, I too had chosen that same path. But my goal was to find Him in all his fullness, a fullness I had found at last in Orthodoxy, thanks to Sophia Mihailovna who had cared enough to open its door to me.

My great friendship with this servant of God did not, I am happy to say, end with her death on January 18, 1972. It has continued, as wonderful and as mysterious as ever as I come slowly to understand a little bit better the endless spiritual struggle which is our common lot as fallen creatures, redeemed by Christ. I think I can now also begin to grasp a little bit better why she too pursued that same spiritual struggle at such great cost, not wishing to miss the only prize worth coveting, Jesus Christ Himself.

Thus when, on her death day, or on her birthday or name day (old or new calender--both seem valid) she surprises me by sending a new friend or an unexpected letter of great spiritual import, I glance at her portrait with a thoughtful, quick smile, that same mysterious smile of total recognition I saw pass over her face when *"very strange happenings"* occurred between us. Crossing myself, I brush away the inevitable tears that, from the beginning have always accompanied her presence, and my heart burns once more from recognizing that she is still standing beside me, as severely as on that first day in Paris, not saying a word, yet there, sent by God.

-- William Bush

MORE FROM REGINA ORTHODOX PRESS
CHECK OR CREDIT CARD INFO A <u>MUST</u>!
BUY 5 ITEMS OR MORE *SAVE 40%* ON

BOOKS/BIBLES

#_____	THE TRUTH	$22.95
#_____	THE THIRD MILLENNIUM BIBLE	$45.00
#_____	THE NON ORTHODOX	$19.95
#_____	TWO PATHS	$22.95
#_____	THE SCANDAL OF GENDER	$22.95
#_____	ETERNAL DAY	$22.95
#_____	THE FAITH	$22.95
#_____	THE WAY	$22.95
#_____	THE MYSTERY OF THE CHURCH	$22.95

CD ROM'S

#_____	HOLY WEEK	$45.00
#_____	PILGRIMAGE TO MT ATHOS	$45.00

VIDEO TAPES

#_____	THE DEFENSE OF ORTHODOXY	$59.85
#_____	ORTHODOX EVANGELISM	$29.95
#_____	PERSONAL JOURNEY - ORTHODOXY	$19.95
#_____	TRUE STATE OF THE UNION	$19.95

MUSIC CD'S

#_____	GATES OF REPENTANCE	$19.95
#_____	FIRST FRUITS	$19.95
Subtotal		$_____
MA residents add 5% sales tax		$_____

BUY 5 ITEMS OR MORE *SUBTRACT 40%* $_____

Add 10% for shipping (Non-USA 20%) $_____

GRAND TOTAL $_____

NAME _____

ADDRESS _____

CITY _____

STATE _____ ZIP _____

E-MAIL _____

PHONE _____

MC or VISA # _____ exp. _____

SIGNATURE _____

REGINA ORTHODOX PRESS PO BOX 5288 SALISBURY MA 01952 USA

TOLL FREE 800 636 2470 Fax 978 462 5079 non-USA 978 463 0730 \

QUESTIONS??? www.reginaorthodoxpress.com